RIBALD TALES
—— OF ——
YESTERDECADE

HASLYN PARRIS

www.trafford.com

North America & international
toll-free: 1 888 232 4444 (USA & Canada)
fax: 812 355 4082

Contents

PROLOGUE

There was a practice, during the late 50s and early 60s at UCWI, Mona, called "shit talk", or ST for short. It was the practice of talking apparently eruditely for long periods about inconsequential and often vulgar topics. The language and argumentation used were deliberately pretentious, pompous, and provocative.

The presentation of these tales is quite deliberately made primarily in that style. Not only does it suit the content of what is to be told, but also I have found it the best style for telling dirty stories to people who wish to be thought of as well-bred, well-read, and polite. These people probably comprise the majority of functionally literate mankind. It is at the Guyanese subset of them that this book is unapologetically aimed.

The stories are not really made up by me. They are all based on fact, garnished for the telling by me, as all tellers of stories ought to do. Many are multiply garnished since they were originally told to me by my friends—but through the multiplicity of garnishing there has persisted the allegation that they are basically true.

Readers should recall, however, that *"is not one dog name Pompey"*, and that this world is full of peculiar coincidences and similarities. **If, therefore, by virtue of what you know, or think you know you find that characters and behaviour patterns in these tales remind you of the living or the dead, please be assured that the kernel of facts around which the stories are built is not adequate evidence to pinpoint any persons you know.** Neither malice, nor historical or geographical accuracy is a characteristic of these tales. It is all "Shit Talk"! **Pure unadulterated, ST!**

But the topics with which the tales deal are only superficially inconsequential. They derive from the complexities and paradoxes in which day-to-day life abounds—complexities such as those deriving from the fact that "chastise" and "chaste" have the same linguistic origins for reasons other than mere coincidence; that there is a peculiar prison designed for women by the juxtaposition of societal values related to virginity, respectability, age, and marriage; that older "happily" married men of high social status not infrequently seek soul-mates among much younger women often of lesser status; and that whores may be necessary pariahs.

These, and other similar matters, are dealt with in these tales in a "sideways" manner, evoking laughter and tears not only of pure amusement.

IN
PRAISE
OF
A

PO

POSY
POTTY
CHIMMY
GROUND THUNDER
WAR CAP
MISS MARY

INTRODUCTION

In Praise of a PO

It is not possible to live for very long in this world without coming to the conclusion that it is far too often an unfair world. Jamaicans have a saying which captures the idea in its complete complexity: ***"Donkey say de world not level—only four o' he feet does touch the ground."*** That predisposition to unfairness applies not only to people, but also to inanimate things. It is a world of savage inequities.

Compare, for instance, Gold with a Chamber Pot.

Gold has acquired a special place of desirability primarily on the basis of its looks, scarcity and durability, rather than of its usefulness. True, in recent times gold had played a unique part in the technology of computers and of space travel, but this 'usefulness' cannot by itself account for the place gold has assumed in our minds and consequently in our language as related to anything eminently desirable.

Thus, for instance, if one can be dull enough to remain married to the same person for fifty years, that dubious "achievement" is celebrated as a **golden** wedding anniversary. If a very good opportunity arises it is described as a **golden** opportunity. If a person persists in being extraordinarily helpful to and tolerant of his fellow human beings, despite their natural tendency to exhibit the most base traits, then one is deemed to have a heart of **gold.**

And when a singer records a song that appeals enough to the lowest common denominator of musical appreciation so that it sells a million records, that singer is awarded a **gold** record. A woman who is sensible enough and pragmatic enough to specialize in dispensing her favours in exchange for material gain only to those men who have access to large sums of money is referred to as a **gold** digger. A source of great profit is described as a **gold** mine. Even the Catholic Church approves— the Legenda Aurea (the **Golden** Legend) by Jacobus de Voragine is a celebrated mediaeval collection of saints' lives.

But no such luck or reputation for the chamber pot! No accolades for it. Its existence is not even easily acknowledged in polite conversation when if it must be referred to it transforms into "potty", with apologies to all listeners. Yet the common or garden PO is a formidable object, properly claimant to involvement in some of the most important aspects of human existence.

I can identify at least seven uses for a Po:

- As a Chamber pot, permitting access to relief without long trips to the bathroom from one's bed at night;
- As a test of virginity and a measure of how far removed from it a young woman is;
- As a defender of chastity;
- As a vital part of the armoury for household security;
- As a bidet, costing far less than the standard ceramic bathroom accessory;
- As a flower pot, especially when wear and tear preclude it from being used otherwise; and
- As a protector of kitchen gardens (a surrogate for a scarecrow) and simultaneously as a target for practice for boys' slingshots.

True. Many a po has come to an unhappy end, disposed of by being tossed into the nearest trench—a vile, ungrateful, and inglorious requiem for an object that had been so closely associated with the tenderest of private parts. But life is unfair! The following suite of five stories sets out to sing the praises of the genus PO, in celebration of its usefulness and its intimate place in the lives of many of yester decade, and not a few of current times.

THE WICKEDEST LITTLE BOY

Both Shakespeare, from the lofty pinnacle of poetic licence, and Mr. Todd, from the depths of uncaring about syntactical rectitude, would have described Lionel as "the wickedest boy." Both Mr. Todd, the farmer who lived across the road, and Mrs. Moses, the Jamaican woman who lived next door, had often faced the complexity of trying to fathom the reasons for Lio's actions. Neither had succeeded in deciphering the workings of this eight year old's mind—but both had experienced the results of its machinations.

Perhaps Lio's parents had contributed in no small manner to his behaviour. As an only child, he enjoyed a very special relationship with a mother who doted on him, and a schoolmaster father who, perhaps misguided by "modern" theories of child rearing, would flog Lio for two and only two categories of misdemeanor—telling an untruth, and stealing. Lio understood this clearly, and the world of mischief was his oyster, safe to explore provided he did not breach the two rules of honesty.

Whatever the reasons, Lio became expert at lateral thinking and a staunch proponent of the scientific method of enquiry; although he himself did not think of his actions in those terms. In a village where all adults appeared agreed that life was generally humdrum, except for the exciting prospect of who next would get pregnant for whom (and there was a lot of that going on), Lio's approach stood out as a beacon of the unconventional. He found excitement in the most commonplace. His mind seethed with a spirit of enquiry based on experimentation; and the subjects of his experimentation derived from the most unexpected juxtapositions of ideas.

Lionel's was the era when DDT was respectable. He was fascinated by the effects of it when the public health authorities came to the village to spray homes—to help eradicate the mosquito nuisance, so they said. Neither he nor Mrs. Moses really knew anything about *dichlorodiphenyltrichloroethane*, but this they did know—when the room in which DDT had been sprayed was deemed safe to be re-entered after the men had sprayed, all kinds of creepy crawlies literally came out of the woodwork. Cockroaches, centipedes, scorpions, all dropped dead on the floor. Who would have imagined that those guys had been living quite comfortably with the people in the house all along?

Of them all, the cockroaches fascinated Lio most—they seemed to be the ones that took longest to die, and they certainly existed in the greatest profusion.

The reward for their resilience as a species was that they became the subject of collection by Lio for further examination. He soon figured out how to catch live cockroaches, and kept his prizes in a paper bag, with the mouth tied with thread he got from his mother—not that she knew that it was cockroaches in the bag.

Lio soon ascertained that cockroaches were peculiarly resilient. They were not easy to drown in water. They seemed to live for long periods without food. When you put your ear against the paper bag containing the roaches, they sounded like a whole mob buzzing and scrambling inside.

And then the idea came to Lio.

It must have done so because Mrs. Moses' largest ram goat was his friend. He had a way with animals, and though the yard was fenced, the paling staves were more for marking off land space than for restricting passage, so Mrs. Moses' goats used his yard as a short cut to get home.

Animals have a way of following the shortest route from A to B, even in the cases where human beings would find it mathematically difficult to calculate such a route. The huge ram goat was a frequent traveler through the yard and became Lio's friend. Even the dogs in the yard understood that and never attacked Mrs. Moses' ram goat, although if they had that goat would probably have given a better than adequate account of himself. Lio had seen the big ram frolicking with the younger rams, leaping up into the air and landing with a crash of horns on the younger ones, especially when it was going to rain. When the goat did this it always seemed to be very happy.

Lio decided to make the ram goat happy. He called the goat, which came to him as a friend, rubbed its tummy and got it to lie down, and then tied the paper bag full of cockroaches around the ram goat's huge balls.

Initially, little happened. But gradually, as the cockroaches clambered around in the bag, the goat became more and more agitated. In short order, the goat was prancing higher and higher, bleating louder and louder, and finally it took off at a dead run for God knows where. It must have been very happy, like Mr. Todd when he was drunk, because it did not run through the usual hole in the fence. It knocked out a paling stave and went its merry way.

Neither Mrs. Moses nor Lio saw the ram goat for about a week, and when Lio did see it, it had seen him first and stayed a great distance away from him. The remnants of the paper bag were still around his balls, so Lio lost both his collection of cockroaches and a friend. He never could understand why the goat would shun one who had made him so happy.

This episode with the goat was by no means the first or the last bit of experimentation in which Lio indulged. Other experiments involved, for instance, testing the hypotheses that cats have nine lives and always land on their feet, by tossing his mother's pet cat several times through the window to see whether it would land on any other part and survive. In time he lost the cat as a friend in the same way he had lost the ram goat's friendship. Neither would come anywhere near to Lio.

With the dogs, the issue was a seasonal one. There was the mystery of why dogs *"fastened"* as part of the activity of mating. No older children, or adults with whom he dared raise the matter, could give a satisfactory explanation. Lio therefore proposed his own reason—It surely was lack of lubrication, and the best lubricant he knew was water. But the dogs would not stand still long enough for him to pour water on the stuck parts, even though he was clearly out to help the slut which was usually being unconscionably dragged by the bigger bull. This problem was resolved by throwing them both into the trench.

All these were well meaning attempts to help. They involved no malice. No more than there was evidence of any suicidal tendency when he had jumped off the top stair of the back steps with his mother's umbrella to see if it would act as a parachute. The fact the bones of the frame bent backwards, and he hurt himself was not a result he had predicted or even anticipated as a possibility.

There was however, some evidence of malice in two other escapades. One was when he had plucked a set of feathers from his mother's favourite fowl cock, and burnt them just when Mr. Assay was visiting, to see whether it was true that burning feathers would make a man's godee roll. He had overheard, and could see from the size of the crotch of Mr. Assay's trousers, that Mr. Assay had a hydrocele.

THE VIRGINITY MEASURE

Perhaps the basest of human traits is the undiluted desire to have something that no one else has, in a situation where they could have it. The principle applies to things which you can acquire, often in competition with others. The possessive adjectives of all languages are all designed to treat with this desire and its satisfaction; and the norms of many societies represent certainly man-made but alleged God-approved rules related to acquisition, possession, and retention.

It is to a large extent this principle which underpins monogamy, prohibits adultery, and inhibits promiscuity, and all the consequential complexities. (The prohibition related to adultery accidentally came under attack through a typographical error whose mass production led to the inclusion of the statement: **'thou *shalt* commit adultery**' in the so-called Wicked Bible). It is this principle also which attaches high value to virginity in the female, in rank defiance of the fact that there are at least two things that do not depreciate with use. Indeed they both appreciate. They are information, and the sex organs through the acquisition of prowess.

Among the complexities which arise is the question of the acquisition of sexual competence by the male juxtaposed with the preservation of virginity in the female, assuming that competence derives from practice and the blind cannot but lead the blind into the bottomless pit. In my youth, many decades ago, I discovered a mechanism which dealt with the avoidance of the results of this complexity. I discovered that the practice existed of the intended husband being put to sleep for one night in the same bed with the maternal grandmother of the intended wife. During that night he was tested by granny in the matter of sexual competence, if not prowess. Grandma's verdict ensured that the blind would at worst be led by the half-blind; and the insistence on female virginity could therefore be preserved and reinforced in such a system. With this man-made adjustment, God's laws could be observed for at least one half of mankind.

But despite all the man-made and God-approved laws, and imaginative and pragmatic amendments thereto, the drive for survival of the species in an animal that is always "in season" cannot be always denied. As every parent knows, neither rhetoric, nor fear, nor good intentions, nor continual surveillance, nor physical impediments, is adequate protection against loss of virginity; and these comprise the gamut of what can be attempted. The fall-back position is damage limitation, and that requires a mechanism for knowing as soon as possible when the inevitable has occurred.

One of the most reliable mechanisms, so some claim, is the po!

It is alleged that the racing car driver, Stirling Moss, avoided a conviction for speeding on the motorway by pointing out to the magistrate that at eighty miles per hour the engine of his car sounded the note B-flat. A check revealed that his assertion was indeed accurate; and the discovery was deemed so remarkable by the legal luminaries involved that Moss' word was taken that he could not have been speeding since his car was not producing the right musical note.

A not dissimilar principle of physics (the similarity residing in the theory of sound) holds for the note which an empty po sounds when peed into, and the rate at which the pitch of the note changes. Even the most non-musical ear can perceive the phenomenon.

The only other principle which needs to be added for the early warning system to work is that virgins, even though squatting over a po, pee in a genteel manner, with both the force and the volume of piss being significantly lower than those of their already deflowered sisteren. Virgin daughter can therefore be compared soundwise with non-virgin mother, and in the pitch dark of a still night one can be distinguished from the other. The difference is palpable.

All that is required, therefore, is separate but same sized posies, one for the mother and the other for the daughter, and a concerned father willing to listen.

That's what led to the breakup of Maisie's marriage, the night her husband George heard their dear only daughter, Margo, sounding exactly like her mother—a kind of "Shaaawah" sound as opposed to the more genteel "Peeuweeuwee".

George accused Maisie of gross negligence and dereliction of duty because she had not told him that Margo "was tekkin man". A loud and long fight ensued; and Margo was so ashamed, what with all the neighbours in the yard hearing the argument that night, that she left home and went to live with her boyfriend. Maisie never forgave George for "macoing" the po so closely, and as soon as possible she too left the home. George still lives in the yard, but with no po. Both women carried their declamatory posies with them.

Postscript

I have been reliably informed that George, and all those who share his belief in piss-in-po sounds measuring variances from virginity are scientifically ill-informed. Apparently, the anatomical characteristics of the female genitalia, and the realities of muscle control, together determine that both virgins and non-virgins can make the same range of sounds when pissing in any po. But truth is sometimes stranger than science—ask George!

IN DEFENCE OF CHASTITY

Joe Scantlebury came from Nabaclis, walking west down the train line to Buxton in the early dusk with the setting sun in his face. That was first forty-five years ago, and the occasion was the August Monday public dance at Tipperary Hall, right next door to Church of God, just off the East Coast public road.

By Buxton standards Joe was a small man, just over five feet and just under one hundred and thirty pounds. But Joe was fit—a strong, wiry man with little body fat. That desirable state persisted despite Joe's well known habit of consuming large quantities of gilbacker mettagee, and swank. His metabolism was part of the reason, and his tripartite occupation of fisherman, farmer, and philanderer was the rest—but popular opinion insisted it was worms, and the alleged size of his penis that was sucking him.

His physical fitness was matched by his taste in clothes. A dapper dresser was he, and Jazz, the village tailor and barber, took pride in maintaining Joe in a state of sartorial and tonsorial elegance.

In short, Joe was a "sweet boy" who didn't smoke, drank little, and could empathise with George Bernard Shaw's assertion that *"We have two tyrannous physical passions; concupiscence and chastity. We become mad in pursuit of sex; we become equally mad in the persecution of that pursuit."*—even though he knew nothing of Shaw.

It was this Joe who on that fateful first Monday in August forty-five years ago landed at the Tipperary Hall dance. It was this Joe who spotted Marion at the dance. Marion was statuesque, standing just less than six feet in her bare feet, endowed with two mouthfuls each of firm breasts, and two handfuls each of firm buttocks. All this Marion carried around on a fine brown frame. Joe's heart sang with prurience, and refused to be daunted by the disparity in size. He had to have Marion as his very own.

To cut a long story short, Joe got into a fight for dancing too close to Marion with his head cradled in the cleft of her breasts while the band played *"I'm in the mood for love"*; beat up his much bigger attacker who claimed Marion was his woman; and thereby earned the right to take

Marion home after the dance. Joe had known that Buxton men didn't like outsiders fooling around their women; but this woman Marion was worth his breach of the Tipperary convention.

So began a whirlwind courtship, primed with memorable goodnight kisses and consummated on a back step of a house deep in Buxton backdam on a dark August Monday night forty-five years ago.

On the long walk back to Nabaclis along the train line that foreday morning, Joe resolved to get married, and by 31st August that year Joe and Marion were wed. He became an honorary Buxtonian, and lived with Marion in Buxton backdam not far from Marion's parents' home.

The marriage had all the signs of being a long and fruitful union. Marion, with a typical mature woman's intelligence and consequent indulgence, never quarreled with Joe about his philandering. In any case she could understand it. She herself found Joe an energetic, hardworking otherwise model husband, attentive to her every need, and decidedly physically satisfactory and eminently sexually satisfying. She knew, with a satisfaction of intimate knowing, whether the popular rumours about the reasons for Joe's slimness were accurate. And in those days there were no organizations of women's libbers railing against the asymmetry of a system of chaste wives and philandering husbands.

That is why, even when she suspected that Joe was 'interfering' with her younger sister, Sister Baby as they called her with a typical fond reversal of the two words that described her relationship with Marion, she made no fuss.

Sister Baby was not as good looking as Marion, but she too sure had a fine brown frame, with tits and butt to match.

But man appoints, and God disappoints. Marion took ill, and not all of Joe's energies and prayers, nor all the doctor's attention prevailed against the call of the grim reaper. On her deathbed, Marion commended Joe to the tender loving care of Sister Baby, died with a smile on her face, and left Joe and Sister Baby with the task of overseeing the twenty year old twin daughters she had borne Joe. They too had fine brown frames.

Joe was desolated by this turn of events; and even Sister Baby's fondest ministrations could reverse the sourness that gradually contaminated his previously ebullient demeanour. Over the next five years the rot really took hold. Joe still worked hard, but he became crotchety, and suspicious. Sister Baby, who had moved into the house ostensibly to help with the household chores, could not cope with the pressures of Joe's personality change.

She let herself go, certainly ate too much too frequently, and soon became so large and bloated that she could not sit on a po and had to resort to a "slab can". A "slab can" is a large enamel bucket with a wire handle that is a surrogate for a po—a slop bucket. Its wider mouth allows it to accommodate larger backsides, but the sharp edge demands some expertise and strength of thigh if you're not to cut your arse when you use it. All this helped infuriate Joe who no longer found her physically attractive. Sister Baby had become just a fat, sloppy, *'red ooman'*.

There is a Jamaican saying: *"Tief no like see tief carry long bag".* It described one of Joe's problems completely. He could not abide any young men coming anywhere near his two beautiful twenty-five year old twin daughters. He even raised an almighty fuss when they wanted to go to August Monday dances at Tipperary Hall. He would come to the train line at night, sit in the nearby rum shop, and wait to meet them on their way back home to the house in the backdam. Any escorts were thanked at that point for their kind intentions to accompany the young women home, and sent on their merry way.

But times had been changing, and so had Joe who now drank much more. Sister Baby prevailed on him to abandon the practice of playing chaperon to grown women, shaming him into agreeing by reminding him of his days, asking why he could not trust the girls whom she had helped bring up in the best Catholic traditions, and pointing out that he was destroying his daughters' prospects of marriage by presenting interested young men with a drunken irascible father. Which of these arguments worked is difficult to say; but Joe abandoned his practice of waylaying his daughters on their way back from dances. He even gave up objecting to their going to dances. For all this he extracted from Sister Baby a commitment that she would assume responsibility for the girls not breeding before they got married.

Sister Baby considered the new task, and together with the daughters worked out a strategy. It was simple. It consisted of her extracting a promise from the daughters that they should bring home any young men who showed an interest, and not indulge in any sexual hanky-panky outside the home. Since Sister Baby was always home, she reasoned that spot checks on visitors would put her in control of how much went on. The daughters agreed because this gave them much more freedom to socialize. A pact had been struck. And then Sister Baby bought a large po which she insisted the daughters use every night before they went to sleep.

And so it came to pass that Pablo and his sidekick Sonny came down from the bauxite town of McKenzie by the boat R. H. Carr to go to the August Monday dance at Tipperary Hall. They stayed in Georgetown until about seven o'clock that Monday evening, and arrived in Buxton by taxi around eight. The dance was in full swing. Synco was in its musical prime and sax was kicking dust. Swinging sax, wailing sax, loving sax, playing all the most loved popular tunes as though they themselves had composed them.

Pablo and Sonny were dance giants, versed in all the most recent dance steps which they had picked up from the cinema. Soon, Tipperary Hall was like a show in the big band era, just like in the films, with Pablo and Sonny as the star dancers. People lined the walls and gave them space on the floor just to see them dance. They rose to the occasion, the band rose to the occasion, and they danced like they'd never danced before in the spotlight of five Coleman gas lamps. Thunderous applause greeted the end of the number. It was applause for the musicians; it was applause for the women with whom Pablo and Sonny had been dancing, but most of all it was applause for Pablo and Sonny who had taken Tipperary by storm. The Buxton men were buying them drinks, and the women hoped that when the intermission ended either Pablo or Sonny would ask them to dance. No problem here with dancing with Buxton men's women.

It was Pablo who first spotted Joe's two daughters. He stopped in mid drink of rum and coke, grabbed Sonny, and said softly *"Jesus"*. What had happened to Joe when he first saw Marion was happening to Pablo and Sonny when they first saw Joe's two daughters. They had fine brown frames.

The intermission ended, a soft slow love song began to be played, and Pablo and Sonny made a bee line for Joe's two daughters. They danced that number, and the next five—all slow sexy ones. Pablo tingled with excitement at how the muscles in the small of the back of his partner rippled as he pirouetted with her around the dance floor, and at how she smiled boldly at him as they danced. Sonny seemed to have found his own reasons for similar delight with the sister. It was settled. Pablo and Sonny would propose that they escort the girls home, and the pair were as pleased as punch when the girls conferred with each other and then agreed.

On the pretext of stepping outside for a breath of fresh cool air, the foursome began the trek to Buxton backdam. It soon dawned on Pablo and Sonny that they had been walking for some time, getting into darker and darker terrain, and so they asked the question about how much further they had to go. Pablo knew Buxton, but Sonny, the less adventurous of the two, did not. A feeling of disquiet took hold of Sonny, but Pablo pooh-poohed his fears, even when he nearly broke his ankle in a hole in the dark road. The girls assured them that they were nearly there, just as the rain began to drizzle.

Rain in Buxton is a funny thing. In minutes it can drench you, and turn the road on which you are walking into a dangerous quagmire capable of safe navigation only by those who know the holes in the road well. To the stranger at night, there is no more formidable task than to find one's way in the dark on the rainy road to the backdam. But if you are arm in arm with a beautiful woman who knows the way, and whose feminine warmth and smell provide a pheromonal distraction from your just fears of losing your way, who cares? So they hurried into the house in the backdam, accelerated not entirely by the prospect of being drenched were the drizzle to become a downpour.

Sister Baby greeted them at the door by the light of the kerosene lamp, and showed them into the small sitting room. Though it was relatively early, only nine thirty (death news was just coming over the small battery radio) Joe was already asleep. His snores could be heard distinctly coming from a bedroom somewhere at the back. Sister Baby asked Pablo and Sonny about themselves while the girls changed into house clothes, and discovered that they were respectable gentlemen likely to be of some means since they worked with the bauxite industry. In any event their clothes reminded her of Joe in his heyday, so they obviously were OK as suitors—but she'd keep an eye on them anyway. She offered them some home-made drink, and the girls returned while she went to the kitchen to fetch it.

The four made small talk while they waited for Sister Baby to return with the drink, but it was enough time to ascertain that Pablo and Sonny had to leave shortly to get transportation back to Georgetown. Sister Baby heard this last part of the conversation as she returned with the drink, and as the drizzling rain suddenly changed into a most ferocious downpour. In a house with a zinc sheet roof such rain always sounds worse than it really is, but even so, this was clearly a serious downpour. It showed no signs of stopping soon.

It was these circumstances that led Sister Baby to suggest that Pablo and Sonny might have to stay the night because of the weather and their unfamiliarity with the road. Initially Pablo and Sonny demurred, saying that they would manage somehow, but Sister Baby knew better and set about making the accommodation arrangements. These were very simple. The two girls would sleep with her in the bedroom leading off from the sitting room, and Pablo and Sonny could use the sofa and the Berbice chair in the sitting room. She would bring two sheets to protect them from the mosquitoes. So all was settled, and Sister Baby retired to the bedroom with the advice to the girls that they should not stay up too late.

Once Sister Baby left, Pablo and Sonny paired off, each with a sister, one pair on the sofa and the other less comfortably so in the Berbice chair. They pretended to pay no attention to each other, but each pair could see the progress being made by the other. Sonny took his cue from Pablo, who had volunteered for the Berbice chair, when he noticed Pablo's hand slide under the girl's dress as she sat on one arm, and thereafter Sonny engrossed himself completely in exploring the assets at his disposal.

Pablo was in for a pleasant surprise. He quickly discovered that his girl had not only changed the clothes she had worn to the dance, but she had also dispensed with her underwear. She said she had been preparing for bed, but he knew different, and that led to the negotiation about from here where.

The plan was formulated. The two girls would get into bed with Sister Baby, and when Sister was heard to be snoring loudly and continuously, Pablo would first crawl into the bedroom. After he left, Sonny would repeat the manoeuvre.

There was no door to be opened since the bedroom was separated from the sitting room by only a heavy cloth curtain. However, they did have to watch out for the po immediately behind the curtain, since Sister Baby routinely placed it there to give warning about any intruders. It was this use of a po that had given it the name "Ground Thunder" (pronounced 'grun tunda') since the kicking of a po in the still of the night indeed made a very loud noise. Sister Baby was an expert in booby traps like that, as was evidenced by the empty bottles which stood at the windows through which access might be gained to the house by an unwanted intruder. Indeed, bottles were also strung at about head height behind the curtain so anyone entering upright, without knowing where the bottles were would also set off an unholy racket.

Pablo was fully briefed about all this and undertook to brief Sonny. The girls duly retired to bed with Sister Baby, who, assured by the warmth of the bodies near to her, soon fell into a deep sleep with snores giving evidence of her departure into the land of nod, hopefully for a prolonged visit. Joe was by now in the second movement of his own snoring concerto, and going strong.

In the dull light of the turned down kerosene lamp, Pablo simultaneously stripped to his underpants and briefed Sonny who nodded his own understanding of the plan. Anticipation was in the air as Pablo got on all fours and began his stealthy approach to the curtain. He got up to it, poked his head inside, and paused to let his eyes get accustomed to the change from light to pitch darkness.

The rain continued to pour. Sonny hissed a whispered enquiry about why Pablo had stopped, which Pablo ignored, and then Pablo put his right hand forward testing for the position of the po. All well so far. Now the right knee. All well so far. Now the left hand. All well so far. Now the left knee, which also took the head forward in anticipation of a repeat of the crawling sequence. Then disaster! **"Graang"** went the po. **"ah who dah!"** went Sister Baby. **"Meow, Meow, Purr"** went Pablo, who froze in fright, hope, and prayer.

Sister Baby sucked a long suck teeth, swore in most unladylike language how she had no cat, but the neighbour's cat was always after Joe's fish, and congratulated herself on the fact that she had had the foresight to have locked up all the fish in the safe. Pablo trembled. His formerly erect and anticipating penis trembled and lost all its tumescence. Fear, the annihilator of sexual desire, won the moment. Pablo began to perspire. He wanted to piss but knew that was ridiculous. This state persisted for ten un-slappable mosquito-filled minutes, and was relieved only by Sister Baby's return to the baritone key in which she had been snoring before the ground thunder's *"graaang"*.

Then prurience returned. Then clear thinking returned. He now knew exactly where the po was; and so with the care of the cat he had imitated, he circumvented the po, navigated his way still on all fours into the bedroom and almost fainted when he bumped his head into the head of the sister he sought. She was a resourceful woman, as eager as he, and had helped by easing out of the bed onto the floor when Sister Baby had resumed her snoring.

Glory to Man in the Highest! For Man is the master of things. No floor had ever felt so supportive, no thighs so warm and welcoming, no genitals so pulsatingly divine as those which Pablo enjoyed that night. Joy was compounded when the other sister, responding to her own urgency, joined them on the floor in a ménage à trois, forming a sharing trio of ecstasy. But all good things must come to an end, as every spent penis knows, and so with muffled groans and bursting heart, there were two pairs of climactic farewells.

Exit was a piece of cake. Pablo knew the terrain now and even left in a half crouch rather than a crawl—only to face the ire of Sonny bred by his own impatience and unfulfilled desire. *"Why you tek so long?"* Sonny remonstrated testily. Yet Sonny had enough sense to listen to Pablo's advice about the location of the po, and about the efficacy of playing a cat, and to even empathise with Pablo's need for time to recuperate from his fright before he could proceed with his sexual pursuits.

So when Sonny set forth in his own version of a hasty crawl and he hit the po, he "meowed" for all he was worth; and all would have been well had he not followed this in his haste with further movement that placed his hand squarely in the po, full as it was of the two sisters' piss, and let out loudly the very human expletive—*"Oh Shit!"*

That was Pablo's cue to leave the house at a dead run. He could hear Sister Baby hollering *"Cat shit and Pepper"* (that meant Sonny would be in hot shit), and the urgent, scrambling, wake-up and lash sounds coming from the back bedroom where Joe was. Pablo tumbled down the front steps but landed still running.

Fortunately he had had time to dress, and was just reminiscing in a mood of post-coital satisfaction when Sonny struck disaster. Pablo ran through the rain all the way to his sister's house in Friendship, the village adjoining Buxton. He was let in, in the dark, by his brother-in-law: a response to his insistent knocking on the door and his screaming for Brother Bertie as he fended off the dog which was waging its own attack on him. Even inventive Pablo had great difficulty explaining his muddy, sodden state so near midnight when all honest travellers are safe in shelter. But there is a comity of men which operated to save him from having to give any explanation to his sister.

Sonny? Well, the next time Pablo saw him was back in Wismar. He had a long scar on his right hand, and the swelling on his face and the bumps on his head had not quite gone down even after two weeks. He simply refused to tell Pablo how he had got out, and resolved resolutely never again to join Pablo in any escapade.

Postscript

The next day Sister Baby regaled the neighbours with the story of how she and Joe had beaten two thieves, emptied a po of piss on them, chopped one on his hand, and cracked his head with a mortar pestle. She still had the jacket, tie and shoes of one of them, and was considering taking the evidence to the police at Vigilance (which she never did). But none of that story could explain to Joe's satisfaction how each sister, in April of the following year, bore a daughter. They grew up into beautiful young women with fine brown frames.

THE REFORMATION OF JOE GREASE

It was one of those cross streets in the village—two hundred yards of burnt earth surface pockmarked with holes, an acned apology for a road. At one end lived the Postmaster; and at the other an East Indian dispenser, above his large drugstore. That was enough to make the street prestigious; but history determined otherwise. The street derived its prestige from the large two-storied green and white house that was in the middle, an imposing but clearly aged edifice which literally overlooked the connection between the two 'middle-walks' that the cross street joined.

The significance of the two-storied house lay not so much in its size and architectural style, but more so in the fact that it was occupied by three, near retirement, unmarried sisters whose surname was the same as the name of the street. The story was that their paternal great grandfather had owned all the property (then mostly land) along both sides of the street, and had therefore lent his name to the street itself. Two generations of genteel non-commercial life had led to the sale of all except the two-storied house. By and large the descendants of the new owners were not well off, and some were decidedly poor, so the street itself exhibited no uniform standard of material well-being.

Clear poverty nestled side by side with so-soness. In this hotchpotch of housing standards, the green and white two-storied house stood out as an enduring relic of better times. How long it would continue to enjoy this basis of prestige was a matter of great conjecture; since the three sisters were all teachers, members of a profession whose social status was not matched by the financial rewards for its practice.

But the green and white house had its own legitimate claims to relative opulence in that street. It was the only house that had a large rainwater vat, and an overhead tank on a trestle with a hand pump connecting the two. The occupants therefore had no need to keep fetching buckets of water upstairs from the standpipe in the yard downstairs, or from the trench, as all their neighbours did. It also had water toilets upstairs and downstairs, and a septic tank, and bathrooms with both bathtubs and showers adjoining each of the four bedrooms upstairs. This self-contained luxury was highlighted by the skylight on the western side which had stained glass window panes, just like the Anglican Church.

As far as creature comforts went, though one primary school teacher's salary could not manage much, three did manage to finance the acquisition of a Bush brand radio run off a car battery (the battery was charged up every three weeks at the Esso gas station on the public road). And there was a large kerosene fridge, so ice and ice-water could be easily obtained, as the more adult neighbours had discovered; and all the little children nearby knew Friday was icicle day. The four-burner kerosene stove in the kitchen had a large oven in which many a wedding cake had been baked; and Friday meant not only icicles but also a free supply of rock buns for the really small kids nearby.

The three sisters were really liked by the whole street, so much so that nobody referred to them by either their Christian name or their Surname. The familiar forms of address were: Teacher M, Teacher V, and Teacher D; and few knew or cared that M stood for Myrtle, V for Veronica, and D for Dorothy. Everyone knew that they lived in a "nice" house, and were "nice" people; a reputation that was bolstered by the fact that each was a "JP" and routinely registered births in the village, even helping to pick names for the newly born. Among them Teacher M, Teacher V, and Teacher D must have had more than fifty godchildren. Their yard was always full of little children "raiding" the various fruit trees with impunity.

The really sacrosanct part of the house was upstairs. No visitors were ever invited up there, although there was a sitting area in which the three sisters sometimes sat reading or simply looking out on a quiet Sunday afternoon. Reputation wise, there was an aura of opulence and exclusivity associated by all with 'upstairs', although none could honestly claim to have been there.

In fact upstairs was a treasure house of family heirlooms—things of value to the sisters because they had been handed down over the generations and had been cared by each current generation. But by themselves they had little market value. Included in these heirlooms were three identical flowered ceramic posies, kept in pristine condition that belied both their eighty year age and the fact that each was routinely used by each of the sisters. It was their own very private secret as to how they knew which po belonged to whom; but they never got their pos mixed up, except once when that resulted in a flaming row that was itself kept very private. Teacher M hadn't spoken to Teacher D for a week about having used her po—but the matter had been reconciled with Teacher V's help and no rows ever occurred again.

Upstairs had something else of value to the sisters—real privacy. There, they could do what they pleased away from prying eyes, including reading books they would never have admitted to ever having seen. Their library of classical, modern, and popular pornography was extensive. It covered books, paintings, lurid sketches, and pieces of sculpture that would have given the lie to all those who insisted the sisters were typical old maids devoid of any real knowledge of, or interest in, sexual activity. Upstairs was the realm of the truly private part of their lives, and they kept it to themselves.

Cheryl was the twenty-one year young woman who lived at the head of the street opposite the postmaster. Hers was one of the poorer shacks on the street; but none of this had rubbed off on her personality which was a rich mix of vivacity and gullibility. It was the second that led to her spawning three young boys, all half brothers, none of whom knew their father. It was the first that led Teacher D to persuade her sisters to give Cheryl part-time employment as domestic help in the green and white house. She supplemented this small income by selling live chickens, ducks, and eggs at Stabroek Market in Georgetown every Saturday, an arrangement that meant she could just about keep herself and her small brood in food, if not in good clothes.

Cheryl's age and energetic occupation together conspired to endow her with a lissom and slightly voluptuous figure that easily showed, even in the loose worn clothing she used to go selling in the market on Saturdays. This must have played a major part in attracting Donald, who soon began courting her with a weekly Saturday frequency. She knew little about Donald, other than that he always seemed fairly neatly dressed, and that sometimes he would disappear for about a month at a time. He never spoke about his job, and always steered the conversation towards matters about Cheryl and her personal life, a tactic which flattered her.

And so, when Donald proposed marriage, Cheryl eagerly embraced the prospect of this caring young man becoming her very own legitimate paramour. Their wedding cake was baked in the oven in the green and white house, and given her relationship with the sisters living there, so were all the patties and other pastry that were served at the small wedding reception. There was no formal honeymoon; but Donald did stay at home and away from work for about a month during which he devoted all his physical attentions to Cheryl. She still was unclear where he worked, but from time to time he would return home with little things for the house, or for the children, or for her. Her impression was that he freelanced, doing job work as he could get it. But sometimes he would disappear in the same way he did during the courting period for two months at a time.

She had given up asking him questions about these disappearances.

Often, Donald would ask her about the green and white house, how well off the sisters were, how well appointed the house was, and things like that, and Cheryl, eager to add to her own importance by association would garnish her accounts as her imagination and mood dictated.

Then one dark rainy night Donald said he had to go out to work, and left with a large canvas bag. Cheryl had never seen the bag, but assumed it must have contained tools that Donald used from time to time, and that he must have got a job that would pay time and a half for working at night.

Donald headed down the cross street, was quickly swallowed up in the dark of the night, and in a short while was standing quietly in the downstairs of the green and white house. He quickly stripped to his shorts, and reaching into the canvas bag took out a large ovaltine tin of Vaseline. He covered his torso, arms and armpits with the Vaseline, ensured that the front door of the house was slightly ajar to facilitate a hasty retreat if that became necessary, and proceeded to mount the stairs to the area of the house where all the valuables were supposed to be. Now he was going into strange territory since Cheryl had been totally unable to tell him anything useful about the layout upstairs.

She had even been unable to tell him that the third treader before the top of the stairs creaked loudly when one stepped on it; or that the sisters slept in separate bedrooms; or that they each had powerful five-cell torch lights which they kept at their bedsides; or that they had a rehearsed plan of action of how to deal jointly with an intruder whom they would always presume to be male.

Teacher D once had a boyfriend whom she had allowed to fondle her; but he had done it so roughly and inexpertly that he had inflicted severe pain, enough to put an abrupt stop to the fondling, and for her to relay the experience in lurid detail to her sisters. Of all things in this world that thenceforth they feared most, it was rape. They had decided that the most valuable thing upstairs was their virginity, and their plan of action was designed to protect this most valuable of assets.

Rape was the act furthest from Donald's mind, and if it had occurred to him it would not have been in relation to three nearly retired women. But perceptions and intentions were what they were; so as Donald opened, entered, and closed the door at the top of the stairs, ready to reconnoitre and size up what valuables were hidden up there, the most bizarre scene was acted out.

Three powerful torchlight beams shone in his face and momentarily blinded him. His greased, naked, torso and near nakedness galvanised the sisters into action with fear. Donald froze in wonder and fright as he saw a woman dressed only in long yellow drawers, advance towards him with full breasts swinging, torch in one hand and po in the other. He could barely think before a deluge of piss hit his face. Before he could recover from that, there was the most excruciating pain in his groin. His balls had become a centre of grief as a mortar pestle landed squarely between his legs. Two more impacts, one on each temple almost simultaneously, left his head ringing and his vision blurred, and his nostrils were filled with the ammonia of yet more piss. His mind said run; but his limbs would not obey. His legs gave away and he collapsed on the floor, only to find himself pinned there on his back with one heavy half-naked woman perched on his belly, another in the same state of undress astride his throat pounding away at his head with a po so hard that the po cracked, and he lost consciousness as the third woman delivered another almighty blow to his crotch with the mortar pestle.

Morning came and Donald found himself neatly trussed up downstairs, bound hand and foot with a clothes line. His canvas bag and his clothes were neatly placed next to him, and three women were calmly keeping a watchful vigil. The sisters had got worried, thinking they had killed him when he had remained unconscious for so long; but Donald was not to know that. From bruised lips he begged to be let go, and not to be reported to the police. He promised he'd do anything they wanted if they'd let him go.

The three sisters retired upstairs to consider the situation. Teacher D was the most adventurous, and it was she who suggested that they employ him as a gardener / handyman with no pay other than meals, since they all knew Cheryl and wanted to avoid her embarrassment. Teacher V suggested that it might not be a bad idea to have around the house a man over whom they had complete control. And Teacher M, who had wielded the mortar pestle, silently considered that the assets which she had damaged could be put to good use, and therefore simply offered to tend to his wounds were he to agree to their proposal.

Thus Donald was unbound, allowed to dress and go home, and reported to Cheryl that he had an accident last night which he didn't want to talk about. Instead he asked Cheryl whether she could ask Teacher D about the possibility of them giving him a steady job as Gardener/Handyman at the green and white house. Donald got the job. The sisters lost a po and gained a man.

Donald became a docile model employee, so much so that Teacher M, who had assumed the task of tending his bruises and swellings with medications and embrocations obtained from the dispenser at the end of the cross street, would take him into the fourth bedroom to administer to him. He was young enough to heal rapidly, and observant enough to notice the title and content of a pornographic magazine one of the sisters had left open upstairs. So when he indicated to Teacher M that he would like to do for her what the picture in the open magazine portrayed, he knew he was taking a hell of a chance, but had guessed right. Teacher M stood looking at him for a long while and then slowly closed and locked the bedroom door.

Donald's job became a sinecure, and he was soon on the best of terms with all three sisters. Cheryl was pleased.

Postscript

The Postmaster's brother was a policeman stationed in Georgetown. He saw Donald one day when he was visiting the postmaster and informed him that Donald was the notorious petty thief the police knew as "Joe Grease". He wondered whether Joe Grease had stopped stealing. In turn the postmaster informed the three sisters. They thanked him, but assured him that Donald had completely given up his thieving ways and was a valued member of their household staff.

REQUIESCAT IN PACE

Most humans indulge in all kinds of conceit, consciously and unconsciously. One, at least among Christians, is that they are unique as being the only ones with a soul or spirit—a kind of unique, invisible, indestructible, endowment from a creating deity that sets them apart from all other non-human things, animate and inanimate. There is no donkey soul, tamarind tree soul, or Po soul; and no heaven or hell for them.

A not unrelated conceit is the axiom that humans are rational in a manner that other living creatures are not. Thus, for instance, they will catch and tag fish from a lake, as part of a methodology for estimating the number of fish in the lake from future catches, never considering that the fish might hold a meeting on the matter with their brothers and sisters with a view to not being caught again. Is this not what humans might do if a Martian fished some of us off the earth, stuck irremovable tabs in our left ears, and then put us back where they had caught us?

And then there are the cruelties in which we indulge in pursuit of various sensual pleasures. These too are often based on our conceits. For example, we look at flowers on a tree, deem them to be beautiful, cut them off the tree in their prime, and take them into our homes to watch them wither and die slowly in the water-filled vases we prize. What if a tree, enamoured of a maiden's breast, were to cut it off with a swinging branch, and stick it on the highest leaves so all the tree could admire it; or, intrigued by the penis of some man peeing against its trunk, were to similarly detach the organ and display it for less lucky shrubs to envy?

But these conceits reach the very zenith of vanity and insensitivity when we deal with inanimate objects. These objects are presumed to have no perceptions, no feelings, and can be totally ignored, or used, or abused as we please. And we learn this from childhood. Their value derives almost only from the market place, all economics, no morality, but some misplaced aesthetics. Our perceptions, and the practices derived therefrom, are reinforced by the inability of the inanimate objects to communicate with us, or to retaliate in a clear physical manner.

As psychologically impoverished entities we need this axiomatic ascendancy over inanimate things. That's why computers frighten the bejesus out of so many of us—they are progressively threatening the ascendancy over the inanimate that we need to live with ourselves. Our very notion of personal privacy demands this assumption of superiority and control.

Let us waive the assumptions about the inanimate for a while and have a quick look at the personal difficulties and complexities that would arise.

Assume that the bar of soap with which you wash your tender parts could perceive and voice its perceptions of what you are doing with it when you wash. Assume that the toilet bowl could comment on the wide variety of backsides and genitals brazenly exposed to it. What if your toothbrush could make a frank appraisal of your mouth each morning when you brush, and you were to be told by it what that appraisal was? How would you deal with the rebellion of the rolls of toilet paper—would you allow democracy to prevail among toilet paper rolls? And how comfortable would you be with the baldly stated views of underwear, and panty liners, and tampons, and condoms, and shoes that you make step on dog shit—you who value your privacy, who have learnt to be ashamed of your nakedness as you are of your innermost thoughts, and who are embarrassed to fart in the arms of your lover?

Yet all is not quite lost. Some of us do form attachments to inanimate things, and behave in accord with the "love" we have for them. We know that inanimate things tend to be more reliable than animate ones, particularly people; and if they fail and let us down, at least we are sure that the reason is neither malice nor the cessation of their love for us—both being sources of much pain. We have favourite chairs, and cars, and shoes, and pens, and trousers, and dresses, and earrings, and necklaces, and rings, and perfumes, and suits, and neckties; and treat them with the possessiveness and jealousy that humans often do with objects they "love". But it is a one-way love. We assume that those inanimate things we love are incapable of loving us; so the love we feel is purely the love of possession, a love of the triumph of ourselves for becoming their owners. We still fart on our favourite chair, and allow piss to drip on our trousers.

But there is enough scientific evidence to suggest that inanimate things often absorb the character of their creators, or their owners; and in any event live a life of their own often in dimensions of time and space not easily accessible by us "superior" human beings.

Betsy, the po, had such a life. Not many posies even have a name, and that is par for the course for most inanimate things. But Betsy did, for she occupied a special place in the heart of her last owner, Miss Mary.

But now, Betsy was on her last journey into oblivion. She had spent five years in the purgatory of the Princess Street trench. Now, some dignitary's impending visit had galvanised the Town Council into trench cleaning action; and the backhoe had dug a lot of rubbish, including Betsy, out of the trench, deposited her in a garbage truck, and that truck was on its way to the incinerator. Rubbish is any inanimate thing that humans no longer want, often because they deem it to be no longer useful. From purgatory to flaming oblivion, losing one's poness forever, transformed into an amorphous mass of twisted metal and dispersed gases. That was the impending transition to Po hell.

Betsy's whole life passed before her eyes, just like humans are always surmising happens just before one dies—that is when one has the opportunity to see death coming.

Betsy's memory bank fast rewound to her first days in Guyana, then British Guiana, a new arrival from England. She had sat in some putagee man's shop in Water Street for two weeks, collecting dust on her smooth white-enamelled skin that had been tastefully decorated with a pastel floral design. There were other pos on the same shelf with her, but something about her made her stand out as a model of elegance, a utensil any lady would be proud to squat upon.

That was twenty years ago, when Miss Mary's mother came to shop near Christmas, and immediately decided to buy it for her eighteen year old daughter. Those were the days when giving an elegant po as a Christmas present was an acceptable practice; so Betsy was acquired on Miss Mary's mother's account with the shop, and the record would show that payment was eventually made in full by March of the next year.

Miss Mary was a beautiful young woman, deserving of a personal po such as Betsy. It was her first personal po. It coincided with her mother also assigning her her own bedroom, in privacy away from her nine year old sister, after her twenty-nine year brother had got married late that year and had gone to live on his own. The bedroom required a few changes to give it a really feminine touch, erasing the masculine aura of her brother's occupancy, and Miss Mary's mother had dealt with that.

It was one of Miss Mary's best Christmases, what with her own bedroom and her own po. A firm bond of love was struck up between the two virgins, Miss Mary and Betsy. Christmas night was the consummation of the relationship when Miss Mary first used Betsy, and also gave Betsy her name. Betsy, for her part remembered the event clearly.

Miss Mary had carefully lifted Betsy out from under the bed that night, had raised the back of her pink nightgown, and had gently placed her smooth, firm, plump and dimpled bottom on Betsy's rim. Betsy barely had time to notice that Miss Mary had a ring of downy hair around her anus, when, with almost loving care, she had let go a gentle stream of warm urine aimed at Betsy's side from between long haired, smooth vulva. Betsy loved the feel of Miss Mary's bottom, and marvelled from her vantage point at the smoothness and firmness of Miss Mary's hirsute genitals. The stream of urine had come in three phases—an initial long main movement, a da capo of almost involuntary drops, and a short coda. Short, sharp contractions of Miss Mary's anus punctuated the phases, as if her arse was taking deep breaths in between her ejections of piss. Betsy would later learn that this would always be the way Miss Mary pissed.

Miss Mary had arisen with a sigh as gently as she had descended. The two halves of her squatting bottom closed as she rose, and the hair covered genitals were hidden from Betsy's sight. Two very small drops of urine trickled down the inside of Miss Mary's left thigh as her raised nightgown descended. Equally gently and even more carefully Miss Mary replaced Betsy, now bearing her first precious portion of warm urine, under the bed. Such had been their first meeting and Betsy fondly remembered it.

The next morning, just before dawn, Miss Mary had taken Betsy to the outhouse in the backyard, and emptied her. Betsy was pleased about this since she had worried that the smell of ammonia that was developing would be hard to endure. To make matters even better, Miss Mary on her return to the house washed out Betsy with sweet smelling soap, and carefully checked that she smelled sweet and clean before putting her back under the bed. Throughout that day Betsy luxuriated in the feeling of belonging to a caring mistress; and neither the darkness under the bed nor the mosquitoes which buzzed around her represented much cause for dissatisfaction.

That day was Boxing Day, and Betsy could hear Miss Mary discussing with her parents that she would be allowed to go with her boyfriend Peter to the party at the Henry's house; provided they were back by midnight. In fact Miss Mary came back just after eleven, Betsy knew, because she had heard the clock chime eleven just before Mary had put her shoes under the foot of the bed. Betsy could hear Miss Mary changing into her nightgown, putting down the mosquito net, and was a little surprised when Miss Mary, having taken Betsy out from under the bed, left the room.

She returned with a kettle, promptly poured water into Betsy, making her almost three-quarters full, and returned the kettle to the kitchen. The water was warm, warmer than urine, and Betsy became even more puzzled when in the dark room Miss Mary removed her nightgown, and then squatted on Betsy's rim. Miss Mary produced a cake of soap, and gently began to wash her genitals with the warm soapy water. She used a gentle downward rubbing action with her right hand to start with, letting the warm water drain from high in front, down over her genitals, and dripping off by itself near her arse. This she repeated for a while. But with each repetition the gentleness of her right hand was replaced by a firmer urgency. The urgency seemed to transfer itself first to her left hand, which reached up to squeeze her full, firm left breast's erect nipple; and then to the muscles in her buttocks which began to contract rhythmically.

There was a synchronization of left hand squeezing, right hand rubbing, and bottom contracting that spread to the muscles of her back which arched; and Betsy noticed the vulval and anal spasms that preceded the deep groan and long sigh that Miss Mary suddenly emitted as she simultaneously said "Peter". The whole episode had taken about fifteen minutes, fifteen minutes during which Betsy had feared that Miss Mary would lose her balance which had become progressively precarious, with her rising suddenly from the rim at the end, and then falling back on it.

That night there was no urinating; although the next morning there was the emptying and cleansing. Miss Mary had simply got up, patted herself dry with a towel, put on her nightgown, replaced Betsy under the bed, and gone to sleep under the mosquito net, hugging her pillow extra tight. Betsy was to learn that this ritual would be performed every time Miss Mary returned from going out with Peter; except that sometimes she would neglect to put back on her nightgown. The ritual held even when she had her period; so it must have been important, Betsy concluded, and was proud that she could participate in something which gave Miss Mary such pleasure.

For six years Betsy's life consisted primarily of these two rituals. Except for one night when Miss Mary had both colic and diarrhoea, and that was the first time that Betsy had to accommodate both piss and shit, with accompanying unpredictable farts. The trauma of the triple stream did not diminish her love for Miss Mary, but she did much prefer Miss Mary to watch her eating habits.

Then Miss Mary married Peter, and they left to live on their own. Life did change then. Miss Mary continued to use Betsy for urinating, but initially the genital washing ritual became pure washing. It was followed by Peter getting into bed with Miss Mary; and from under the bed, and above the sound of the bedsprings, Betsy could hear the same sounds Miss Mary used to make, except that now they were louder, more prolonged, and included imploring to God and Jesus Christ in addition to Peter. For his part, Peter too sought the intervention of God and Jesus Christ, and pleaded to Miss Mary; so Betsy concluded that Miss Mary was giving as good as she got, so all was well—there was no advantage. But none of that explained why this happened so many times in any one night. In any event, Miss Mary always seemed chirpy and happy the next morning when she took Betsy to be emptied and cleaned.

Until one morning when Miss Mary retched and vomited in Betsy. Betsy was so taken aback that she nearly jumped out of Miss Mary's hands. After that incident, which was repeated on a few other mornings, Betsy noticed that Miss Mary was becoming heavier, and less dexterous in squatting on her rim. Betsy also noticed that Miss Mary's genitals were looking more succulent. The increase in weight and the other changes continued for several months, and she clearly wasn't having her period anymore.

Then Miss Mary suddenly disappeared, to the hospital they said.

Betsy was distraught. She missed Miss Mary. But within a week Miss Mary returned, with a baby boy they named Jonathan. Then life returned to normal, almost. Betsy never quite forgave Peter and Jonathan for what they had done to Miss Mary's genitals. Not only did they now look distinctly emaciated, but in addition there were some stitches holding together a tear that extended nearly to Miss Mary's anus. In time things healed, but Betsy's opinion never changed.

This state of unforgivingness only worsened when Jonathan reached the stage of being potty trained. He developed the habit of seeking praise from

Miss Mary by taking Betsy to her to show he had used it. And this led to several embarrassments since Jonathan did not care who was around when he wanted to show off. One day, Jonathan had Betsy on his head, just after he had used her, and he tripped and fell on his way to his mother. There was shit everywhere; Betsy sustained a nasty flake on her enamel on her right side just where the pastel flowers were, and could barely endure her chagrin when she realised that everyone was fussing over the little bugger and ignoring completely the damage to her.

They did notice the flake later though, since it developed into a pin hole and the leakage of piss drew attention to it. The cure, however, was worse than the disease. They rectified the situation by melting the tar from a bag that had contained last Christmas' ham, and plugged the hole with the melted tar. That left a large black blotch on Betsy's previously pristinely pure smooth white enamel skin, and Jonathan scorned to sit on Betsy with the black blotch inside. He took to banging Betsy on the floor, generated new flakes which developed into new pin holes, and new plugging with melted tar. The situation became untenable, and even though Jonathan got a small new plastic po that he would use, Betsy's best days were past, and Miss Mary replaced her with a new pale green ceramic po.

Betsy was retired from bedroom service, and never again saw Miss Mary's bare bottom and its interesting environs. She missed the sound of the bedsprings at night, and the voices of Peter and Miss Mary calling to the Lord and each other; but she didn't mind missing the trauma which the new green po had when the bottle of fly under the bed had exploded just before Christmas.

Now Betsy had the role of flower pot near the bottom of the front step. It wasn't too bad once you got accustomed to the mix of cow dung and dirt which apparently the flowering plant needed—ugh! But there was this disgusting, scrawny, hip-shot bull dog which had taken to pissing frequently on Betsy, just to show that she belonged to his territory. Sometimes other bull dogs would pass and dispute his claim, so they too pissed on Betsy, and their piss had to be overruled by the resident scrawny dog's pissing all over again.

And then, seven years later salvation seemed at hand. The resident scrawny dog got run over by a drinks truck. He was however replaced by a pet pup for Jonathan, and that pup must have been related to a farmer. He continually dug out all the soil from Betsy, leaving the flowering plant in shambles. The matter was resolved by Miss Mary finding an entirely new flower pot—a huge concrete affair that the young pup could barely reach into, and certainly could not overturn. Thus ended Betsy's days as a flower pot.

Betsy was transferred to the kitchen garden, upside down on a long pole to play the role of scarecrow. By way of preparation, Peter and Jonathan had painted the outline of a man's face on her, and had completed the transformation by painting large and small black dots all over her outside. She looked like she had got a bad case of po pox; and was condemned to always having her bottom in the air through sun and rain.

The trouble was that the birds she was supposed to scare away soon overcame the fear of her strange appearance, and would calmly rest from their efforts at digging up and eating the seeds in the kitchen garden by perching on top of her backside. Jonathan and his mischievous friends soon noticed this, and used their homemade slingshots to shoot at the birds. Invariably they missed, but often hit Betsy with a resounding "clang" of brick hitting iron. More flakes occurred, and life became more difficult. And it all came to an end when one of them missed so badly that the stone broke a neighbour's glass window.

Peter soundly thrashed Jonathan, and that was good as far as Betsy was concerned, but then he also threw Betsy into the Princess Street trench, without even giving her a chance to say goodbye to Miss Mary. Betsy used to be able to see Miss Mary everyday when she went to the back to empty and wash the green ceramic po, or to hang out clothes, and she could take comfort in the hot sun from her reminiscences.

Miss Mary had got considerably fatter, but Betsy still remembered her fondly. Betsy often wondered whether Miss Mary still had the same bedroom rituals, but she never got a chance to ask the green po.

Betsy was jolted from her reverie by the garbage truck's tray suddenly lifting and emptying its contents into the incinerator. The heat was unbearable. Her remaining enamel cracked, and then she lost her shape as a pretty po. She became an amorphous twisted lump of metal, screamed the silent scream of the abused inanimate; and then the flames carried her to po oblivion.

Postscript

Peter and Miss Mary got divorced around the same time that Betsy got incinerated. If the green po had had an opportunity to speak to Betsy, she would have been able to predict that trouble was afoot. You see, Peter had started sleeping out, and Miss Mary had resorted to the bedroom washing ritual as it originally was—only this time her implorings were to God, Jesus, and somebody named Noel.

THE SAGA OF BOOM BOOM

Thirty-five years ago, a baby girl was born to a young woman who had been two years divorced. One year after the divorce the young woman, the lonely relic of a childless three year marriage that was memorable for its unhappiness had become involved with a roué. He was a policeman, a womaniser, and a hard drinker. That combination made him popular among men and women, but did little to relieve the pressure on the small salary of a policeman, or much to enhance his chances of promotion from the rank of corporal. The involvement resulted in the birth of the baby girl, and the near disappearance of the policeman. All this happened in New Amsterdam thirty-five years ago. The girl was given the unusual name of Vlida.

The little girl had grown up knowing but not knowing her father, and loving her mother and her grandmother with whom she lived in a tenement yard. The main source of income was her mother who made cakes and sold them, catered for high society functions, and did dressmaking for many of the more fashionable women in the town. Theirs was not a life of abject poverty; but it was a frugal life with need often being satisfied with a lag, and want seldom being attended. Her father rarely contributed financially to their overall well-being, his funds having gone primarily into the maintenance of his reputation as a sporting fellow; but he slept in the house and did occasionally contribute something for food. In any event, most of the time he was as tight as a kite.

Vlida wanted to love her father, but it is difficult to love someone whom you see only occasionally, and who when you see them is at least slightly inebriated and prone to fall asleep in the middle of a conversation. Indeed, there were only three clear memories which she had of her father who had left the home when she was six—her mother had requested him to remove himself.

All three memories were traumatic. The first, when she was three, related to him coming home, tight as usual, but earlier than usual in the evening, and finding her dressed only in her little panties entertaining her mother and grandmother by wining to a calypso on the early evening radio. He had flown into a rage, slapped her twice, threatened to skin her alive if he ever saw her dance like that again, and sent her to bed. That episode had a lasting effect on her. She never could, after that, even when she became a grown woman, dance with the sensuous swivel of hips that all the other girls managed with consummate ease.

The second, when she was four, was coming awake in her mother's bed because the mattress was shaking. She had fallen asleep with her mother that night because her father was on night duty. Despite her best efforts she could not get up. The bed continued to shake for what seemed like an eternity. She could hear her mother groaning and sighing softly, and her father grunting in a peculiar sort of guttural way; but her mother was holding her down firmly on the bed in her face-down sleeping position under the sheet. Eventually the shaking stopped, and her mother let go of her. She had sprung up to find her father in the bed with only his underpants on, breathing heavily and perspiring, and her mother looking a little dazed. She had run out of the room to her grandmother's bed, and it was many years before she figured out what must have really happened. Meanwhile, and for all those years, she blamed her father for the whole frightening experience.

The third, when she was six, had to do with the cause of her mother insisting that her father leave the home. He had been complaining that evening about how everyone in the force was against him, because he was more intelligent than they, and more academically qualified than they, and that was why they would not promote him from the rank of corporal. In a rare moment of frankness (perhaps because she had a hard day and was short on patience and goodwill) her mother had responded to the complaints by stating some much more likely and unflattering reasons for his lack of promotion. He had responded by hitting her with his clenched fist; and she had retaliated by hitting him across the face with her rolling pin. The battle ended almost before it had begun. In his dazed and slightly inebriated state he simply stood and stared at her mother, who with no loss of heat and a firmness of voice that brooked no argument ordered him out of the house immediately.

He left that night in unprotesting silence, returned from time to time for fleeting visits allegedly to see his daughter, but never became part of the household again. Eventually the visits diminished in frequency and then stopped, maybe because he felt unwelcome. They never really heard of him again until many years later when his death was announced over the night-time death news. No tears were shed by either mother or daughter.

Vlida was a bright and vivacious little girl. She did not suffer too much from the lack of brothers and sisters, since there were many other children in the tenement yard to play with, and for quite a while she was a little tomboy.

She could out-run and out-climb most of the other children, including ones who were older.

It was during these years that the children in the yard gave her the name "Boom Boom". No one could recall the incident which gave rise to that sobriquet, but it stuck; and even her mother and grandmother called her that. Vlida was a name relegated to use only for official documents.

Boom Boom grew up with three overwhelming influences. The first two referred to feminine hygiene.

Her grandmother was always asking in a loud voice, which invariably embarrassed Boom Boom, whether she had washed her pat-a-cake. The question was asked twice per day, in the morning and in the afternoon, and its answer was usually succeeded by a check that included the state of cleanliness of her teeth, her armpits, and her fingernails. As Boom Boom grew older the loudness of the enquiries disappeared; but all four enquiries and checks themselves persisted; as did the insistence on the use of a blacksage tooth stick, a nenwa scrubber, and lime for the armpits.

The second had to do with the cleanliness and neatness of her clothes, particularly her underwear. All her clothes, including her underwear, were made by her mother. She soon had ingrained in her the habit of daily washing of her underwear, daily ironing of her other clothes, and daily examination and needlework repair as necessary of both. No torn drawers could be worn—a principle which she noticed that some of her mother's dressmaking clients did not faithfully observe.

The third had to do with social status. There was a stream of constant reminders that she had no resident father, but that she was required to be "better" than all other kids if she was not to let down her mother and grandmother. Though she was poor she had to be respectable; and being respectable meant walking "properly", talking "properly", being polite, and not getting into fights.

With these three principles Boom Boom was being groomed for entry to a status higher than her origins, or her environment—a status she was told she deserved. She faithfully absorbed all the lessons, together with the social innuendos and prejudices about her origins and her tenement yard friends.

At primary school Vlida excelled in her schoolwork, but curiously, from the point of view of her teachers, took little part in physical extracurricular activities. They were not aware of the norms of never-to-be-disturbed neatness and cleanliness by which she lived; and therefore could not understand her eschewing the place of prominence that her obvious physical strength, good coordination, and lissomness would have allowed her to assume. Her academic performance led to her going to high school where she did very well at her "O" levels—her first real taste of elitism. It tasted good.

At seventeen, she was an attractive young woman, not yet fully filled out in terms of bust and hips, but with a strong somewhat boyish frame that had clear promise for carrying a statuesque body in its more mature years. Her academic achievements and perpetual neatness made her a role model for the tenement yard children.

But her own social aspirations and prejudices made her unsure of herself when dealing with people from the very stratum of society to which she aspired and her mother aspired for her. She would always need to be reassured that she was indeed worthwhile, quick to perceive slight where none existed or was intended. She was long on aspirations as she was on insecurity, but she kept it all inside her, not even discussing it with her mother and grandmother. Basically she appeared stand-offish, as though she thought she was better than everybody else; but it was really shyness and insecurity at war with aspiration.

This insecurity led to an interesting problem with her manner of speech. She normally spoke in a very low voice, and had great difficulty speaking in public, as for instance when the school required her to give the vote of thanks at her last speech day. But at home in the tenement yard her voice would rise to that of a shrewish screech when she dealt with the lesser beings that inhabited that space. It was the first real indication of what her behaviour would be were she to achieve her aspirations.

Money was a problem; and so while other more financially fortunate girls with academic qualifications less good than hers were proceeding directly to university abroad, or were embarking on "A" levels preparatory to going to university abroad, Boom Boom entered the world of work. She despised the unfairness of it all, and resolved that someday she would really be somebody.

Her own cogitations led her to conclude that she should pursue a career in medicine since that seemed one avenue that would assure her rise to her coveted place in society.

The doctors and the midwives—these were among the people who appeared to live in the best houses and command public respect in New Amsterdam. She resolved to join that group, and so sought and got a job in the largest drugstore in the town.

Over the next seven years, her intelligence, curiosity, diligence, and ambition, combined with access that the owner of the drugstore gave her to his books on chemistry and pharmacology, and his own technical explanations, led to Boom Boom becoming extremely knowledgeable about the non-financial side of the pharmacy business. Indeed, her knowledge was about as good as one could get without attending formal courses, and better, in terms of being up-to-date, than many formally trained practitioners in the medical profession.

Those seven years saw impacts on her personal development in many ways; and these included a peculiar stagnation.

For instance, now that she had some money and access to the knowledge one easily picks up in a drugstore, she made some fundamental changes in her personal habits. Blacksage, nenwa, and lime exited, and were replaced by the best toothbrushes, toothpastes, and feminine deodorants. Her mother's home made pads gave way to tampons and commercially produced pads which she used in accord with the advertised advice. Her still developing breasts were cuddled in more comfortable and better fitting bras than anything her mother could fashion; and were displayed in all their 36 B-cup glory with just the right amount of lift.

After a brief foray into fashionable panties, she maintained a very selective attachment to her mother's home-made drawers, based on the loose comfort they provided, and on the fear of contracting one of those itchy female fungal infections that the literature said are encouraged by persistently wearing tight panties without cotton crotches. She was amazed by the number of "respectable" women who came to purchase creams and ointments to deal with those ailments. In any event, a number of types of the fashionable panties rode up in between one's buttocks; or worse, slipped part-way between the vulval lips—an uncomfortable circumstance not easily corrected without embarrassment in public.

For some time she had been concerned about what she considered one of her physical flaws—her face. She considered it too round, with cheeks that were too fat, and thickish lips that departed too far from the classic Cupid's bow shape favoured by the adverts for lipstick. She blamed this genetic damage on her father. Damage limitation consisted of experimenting with and learning to use make-up tastefully; and particularly to apply lipstick carefully to set her lips off to their best advantage. She emphasized this aspect so much that she would not go out, not even to the market, and certainly not to work without spending at least twenty minutes fixing her face; and there were several checks and adjustments made in the course of the day.

She also developed the routine of having her mother straighten and style her hair every weekend—an activity which her mother had added to her repertoire of activities to bolster the family's money earning capabilities.

In terms of stagnation, Boom Boom became increasingly self centred, developed no real interests outside herself, and no hobbies. She did read her fair share of novels; but her reading was not focused in a hobby sense. She learnt no parlour games, and generally was blissfully untutored in the more sophisticated ways of enjoying leisure. The house of her dreams would not have contained a study; but if it did, she would have seldom used it. She was bright and could learn quickly, but had never developed a taste for scholarship. Learning was a means to an end—social status.

In the four years since she had begun working with the drugstore her physical appearance changed, becoming more sophisticated in the same manner that her mind had been developed in relation to pharmaceutical matters. Nature's blandishments had been enhanced by Boom Boom's own ordered personal efforts, and the now decidedly attractive young woman was getting attention. The attention came not only from clients who respected and sought her advice on purchases from the store, but also from young men who clearly found her an attractive sex object.

This latter group of interested persons she ignored, that is with the exception of John, whom she had known since high school, and whom she considered an ambitious person. John wanted to become an architect, and she respected his strength of ambition. They began dating, with her mother's approval, and soon became very engrossed in each other's career dreams. But John reputedly played around with some other girls and women, so in that one-many situation they remained good friends without becoming lovers.

One evening, John took her out to the cinema, and on their return found that her mother and grandmother had gone to bed. They sat talking in the drawing room with the single dim light bulb, and John confided that he would soon be leaving Guyana to take up a junior job with a leading architectural firm in the USA. It was just the break he needed for his career; but he was hesitating, he said, because he would miss Boom Boom. She was touched by all this, and sought to assure John that she'd be here in NA when he returned from his training. John swore that he loved her, telling her so for the umpteenth time since they had started dating nearly a year ago; and with verbal and physical cajoling managed, among kisses and tentative fondling of her breasts to do something no other than she had ever done—caress her lower tummy and touch her crotch.

Though John had done this discreetly, ready to apologise for the accidental touch if she complained, with his hand on the front of her loose thin dress as they sat in the settee, the pleasant sensation was unmistakable. And, maybe, this is why when she felt him slide his hand under her dress onto her bare thigh she didn't object. She did tense up a little, not quite sure what to expect next, but the pleasant sensation remained and increased. She remembered that she had chosen a skimpy pair of panties that evening, and wondered whether she should have. What would John think of her if he found out that she wore that daring kind of underwear?

She didn't have to wait long for any answers as John's fingers deftly shifted aside the panties and gave John his own great surprise—he had no idea that she had so much pubic hair. It effectively blocked further progress of his hand, and it was only her facilitating movement of slightly parting her things and simultaneously sliding her bottom further to the front of the settee and raising it, that allowed him to reach the goal he had hardly dared to believe possible.

One thing led to another, and in the age old tradition of "striking while the iron's hot", John soon had Boom Boom facing him in his lap, astride him, knees doubled up on the settee, and skirt hiked up around her waist. He'd managed to extract his penis from his trousers and soon his major preoccupation was how to keep Boom Boom quiet as she wriggled uncontrollably with a mixture of pleasure and apparent pain. He was kissing her, as much for the pleasure of kissing as for the necessity of smothering the sounds she was making. He got two things in return—the longest, hardest bite he'd ever had, on his lower lip; and a simultaneous sudden violent thrusting onto and engulfing of his penis. All together they nearly made him faint. He realised that he was no longer in control of the whole exercise. Boom Boom had him locked into a position in which he could not move; and she wasn't moving either—just gripping everything in a vice-like lock.

He was as scared as hell, worried that her mother would emerge to investigate the sounds, but far more worried by the pain he was feeling in his lip and in his crotch where his zip was also squeezing his balls. But he couldn't move—not in search of comfort or in pursuit of stimulation. Boom Boom would not let him. She just held him there. God, she was strong.

After what appeared to be an eternity, Boom Boom sighed and suddenly got up. There was a slight plop as his frightened, flaccid, bruised, un-ejaculated penis was released; and when he looked down he could see a few smears of blood on his briefs showing through his open fly. Boom Boom was standing rigidly still over by the window opposite the settee. There was nothing but dark, deserted tenement yard to see out there; but her gaze was fixed and unwavering.

John got up shakily from the settee, fixing himself, and then standing close behind her he gingerly placed his hands on Boom Boom's shoulders. She didn't relax, nor did she encourage him to embrace her. In a short while she simply turned around, looked him straight in the face, and said quietly and matter-of-factly: *"John, it's late. You'd better go home"*. He left without any further words, quietly letting himself out through the door next to the window. Boom Boom didn't even say goodbye.

She stayed at the window for a while gathering her thoughts. She marvelled at the nice sensations she had felt before they had intercourse; at how the discomfort and sharp pain of penetration had spoilt the whole thing; but most of all she marvelled at the feeling of power she had got when she had held John down and forced him into her and he had been completely in her control—John, who had so many girlfriends, and had a reputation for having a way with women, many far older than her.

She left the window, slowly took off and carefully folded her panties, and placed them at the bottom of the bottom drawer where she kept all things she considered personal and precious. She locked the drawer. Then she went to the bathroom and in the dark slowly and silently did what her grandmother so often asked her if she had done when she was a little child. She was now a woman of twenty-one.

Three days later, John came to the drugstore. He said he'd come to say goodbye since he was scheduled to leave Guyana the next day. Boom Boom had smiled charmingly but without welcoming warmth, and wished him a safe trip. He muttered that he would write soon, and in a quiet unemotional voice she had replied that she'd look forward to receiving his letter. An awkward silence descended. John could find nothing to say so he turned to leave. As he did so she gently touched his arm and said with great feeling: *"Best of luck. I'll remember you"*.

She watched John leave, walking as though he was in a daze, head down and steps faltering.

It struck her that there was so much more she could have said to let him know that she really liked him. She could for instance have made a private joke about his still swollen lower lip about which she knew he had told people that a marabunta had stung him. For his part, John never found a way to indicate to Boom Boom how her pubic hair had bruised the head of his penis. Instead, he had quietly walked away, and she had pensively watched his disappearing back. Somehow, they both knew that the whole thing was more complex than either wished to handle, and that John would never write.

Life went on, and Boom Boom seemed to grow more attractive with each passing month. In her fifth year with the drugstore she was promoted to head up their customer relations department. She had an official title and a small office to go with it. What that meant was that she had to deal personally with all the important customers of the drugstore—the private doctors, small dispensers who bought their stocks from the store, dentists, and even the procurement officer from the Public Hospital. She was tailor-made for the job. Her aloof manner commanded automatic respect, her knowledge of the products inspired confidence, and in financial transactions she was meticulous and scrupulously honest.

It was in her job as customer relations manager that she first came into contact with the dentist, Dr Ng Qui Fook.

She had heard the rumours, discussed by her mother with her tenement yard friends, about Ng Qui Fook liking young brown skin girls like her; but she never had cause to pay too much attention to the matter—at least, not until she had to do business with him. He seemed to want to talk about all kinds of things other than the purchases of drugs which had brought him to her office in the store. She succeeded in redirecting him to discussing the business at hand, and concluded it; but not before he'd asked her out and she had given a polite refusal.

She had refused for two reasons. One was that she didn't like him or his reputation. The other was that she would have been ashamed and embarrassed to have him come to the tenement yard to pick her up for a date. Even though she, her mother, and her grandmother lived in the second house in the yard, she didn't want the other occupants in the yard to see him coming to pick her up. And she had no intention of meeting him at any corner. John was different. Everybody had known John; but Ng Qui Fook was a "big-shot" popular bachelor who could have only one purpose in visiting a girl in a tenement yard. What else would a "respectable" chinee man be visiting for?

Boom Boom had the courage of her convictions and the reinforcement of her prejudices and maintained a resolute "No" to all Ng Qui Fook's invitations. But there was no acrimony. They were on friendly terms—at arm's length.

Then one evening she developed a terrible toothache, somewhere at the back of her left jaw. Her grandmother attributed it to the abandonment of blacksage, salt and chalk, for fancy toothbrush and toothpaste. Her mother, attributing no cause, sought to deal with the more immediate matter of the pain by suggesting that Boom Boom take some aspirin. However, she had been doing so since the previous day when the ache had begun, and the aspirin was not working anymore. A more potent home remedy was clearly required, so her mother examined her mouth, located the offending tooth and made a cotton wool pack laced with formalin to stick into the hole in it.

Initially there appeared to be some relief, but the pain grew worse during the early hours of the morning of the next day. And when Boom Boom looked at her face in the mirror, her already too round face looked like a lopsided balloon. Boom Boom could not decide which hurt more—the tooth or her pride about how her face looked. She resolved to go to a dentist first thing after daylight.

But it was Sunday, and dentists did not work on Sunday. Boom Boom knew there was one dentist who would see her—Ng Qui Fook. She just hoped he was at home where he had his surgery, and had not gone out of town. She bathed in her usual careful way, and faced with the need for as much comfort as possible decided to wear the new light green trap-door drawers her mother had recently made for her—no tight panties today. Trap-door drawers are called that because of the flap which they have in the crotch that when unbuttoned allows one to go to the toilet to urinate with a minimum of undressing.

That day, her need for comfort was so great that she did not even bother to put on a bra but wore a loose blouse instead. Her breasts were firm enough to manage without the engineering support; and she completely abandoned the ritual of fixing her face.

By eight that morning, freshly bathed and minimally but comfortably dressed Boom Boom rattled the chain on the front gate of Dr Ng Qui Fook's house. The dear dentist appeared to be an early riser, and was in his kitchen garden pottering around in his short pants. She noted that he had sturdy well shaped legs, and recalled that he had been some kind of athlete, playing hockey or something like that.

For his part Ng Qui Fook was pleased to see her, but realised that something unusual must have brought her. As he got closer to the gate all became clear—her lopsided balloon face and her impeded speech told the whole story.

Ng Qui Fook invited her into the surgery downstairs, and asked her to give him a few minutes to wash up and change. Within ten minutes he was back, in a new clean pair of short pants and a clean white shirt over it. He put her to recline in the dental chair and set about examining her teeth. As he tilted the chair backwards in the standard fashion he could not help seeing her bare breasts jutting proudly against the thin blouse, especially since the top button of the blouse had come undone. He shivered a little at the beauty of that revelation; but brought his mind back to the professional job he had to do. His mind seemed all right but his crotch seemed to have a mind of its own. Fortunately his erection was hidden behind the chair.

His examination showed that a molar had really decayed, and there would be no alternative to extraction. It might even be that an abscess had formed. He told Boom Boom this, and said that even with the local anaesthetic he would use she would feel a fair amount of pain. All this he said while he still had his instruments in her mouth so it was only the nodding of her head that had indicated her agreement for him to proceed. Boom Boom hated pain, but had concluded that there was no alternative to the extraction.

He administered the injection of the local anaesthetic, and left her a while to allow it to make the area numb. Meanwhile he made small talk with her, trying to put her at ease; but this was the first time she had gone to a dentist, and all sorts of fear were in her heart. No small talk would help. She could feel the butterflies in her stomach, and prayed that she would not fart as she knew she was prone to do when she was really scared.

The extraction began, with her head cradled firmly backwards in the headrest of the chair which had been set to its maximum reclining position. At the first application of pressure from the forceps, Boom Boom felt a pain of a kind she had never felt. It seemed to go from her jaw to the top of her head and down past her crotch to the tips of her toes. She tried to tell him to stop, but with her mouth opened wide she could only get out a gurgled sound. In any case he obviously had a firm grip on the tooth and clearly no intention of letting go until it had come out.

The second pull did it. Toothache or no toothache this confounded nonsense had to stop! Boom Boom's back arched, and using the leverage of the headrest, her hips and thighs swivelled upwards until her thighs were firmly locked around the sides of the dentist's face and her feet clasped behind his neck. The trap-door of the green trap-door drawers was directly under his chin, and Boom Boom was squeezing with her thighs for all she was worth. Ng Qui Fook had never been in a scissors lock of that kind in any situation, and he hoarsely shouted to her to let go—all to no avail.

The obvious solution was to let go of the tooth; but good sense and decency had deserted them both, she driven by excruciating pain, and he by equally compulsive professionalism. The job had to be completed. He braced himself and gave a third pull. A series of things then happened that neither would forget.

Boom Boom's arms joined her feet behind his head and locked tight. Two buttons from the trap-door burst loose. Her succulent genitals stared the dentist squarely in the face, and he could see her tensed abdominal muscles. The heady musky smell sent shock waves through his penis which was now fully erect. Perspiring, he made a final prolonged pull. A stream of hot piss landed on his forehead; and he ejaculated in his pants just as the tooth came free and Boom Boom let out a loud fart.

It was all over. Boom Boom's arms and legs suddenly relaxed and collapsed back down into the chair, freeing Ng Qui Fook, who tumbled off the perch he had chosen on the circular iron ring at the base of the chair in the height of the near-silent battle. The forceps with its tooth clanged to the floor, and Boom Boom's head bent over into her lap where she was emitting blood filled sobs in an uncontrollable fashion. Ng Qui Fook sank down into a dazed, perspiring heap on the floor.

After about a minute, they all recovered enough from the mayhem for Ng Qui Fook to give Boom Boom glass after glass of water to wash the blood out of her mouth. She was totally embarrassed, and he could see that. His own anger evaporated, he started feeling sorry for her, and sought to comfort her with soothing sounds, not making much sense in what he was saying, although it sounded like *"never mind, never mind"* repeated over and over again.

Boom Boom eventually calmed down enough to speak in a hoarse, barely understandable whisper. It was in this whisper that she apologised, cried a little more, and accepted the medication and instructions which he gave her. In almost priestly fashion he absolved her of her sins, and offered to drive her home in his car since she looked such a thorough mess, what with blood all down the front of her blouse and skirt.

She accepted the lift, thanked him when he had deposited her at the gate of the yard, and walked as quickly as she could without running, into her house. Her mother was aghast at the sight of her bloody clothing; but Boom Boom told her not to worry, took the bloody clothes off and asked her to soak them down, and in the privacy of her bedroom took off the green trap-door drawers and placed them in the bottom of the bottom drawer of her chest of drawers, and locked it.

She went to bed and slept for the rest of the morning and most of the afternoon. When she awoke, late in the afternoon, the pain had substantially subsided, and she gave her mother the briefest of explanations about how painful and difficult the extraction had been. Her mother had muttered something about her father having strong teeth, and then quietly gave her the first of the six doses of hourly medication which the dentist had recommended. By the next day the swelling of her face had completely disappeared, and Boom Boom went to work as usual, perfect make-up and all.

Ng Qui Fook had spent the rest of the morning cleaning up his surgery, and otherwise tidying it up. He lived alone, and he spent the afternoon wrestling in his mind with the vision of the genitals which he had been presented with in such unusual circumstances. Just remembering that part of the scene sent shivers of desire through him, and that night he found he could not sleep without masturbating.

The next day Ng Qui Fook visited the drugstore and spoke to Boom Boom about some purchases he needed to make. Neither spoke about the events of Sunday morning, nor did he ever present her with a bill for the extraction. But the way they smiled at each other as he left made it clear that a very special friendship had been established, still at arm's length but special.

Boom Boom remained on Dr Ng Qui Fook's mind as a sex object. He just could not stop thinking about her at the oddest times, even when he was sporting with his friends surrounded by willing, eminently desirable, women among whom he could have his pick for the night. The matter was beginning to interfere with his ability to sleep peacefully at night, and so he resolved to consult the only friend he had whom he could trust to remain silent about it.

He spoke to Dr Rhone about a year and a half after the incident in his surgery.

Dr Rhone was, despite his uncommon name, a Guyanese. He seemed to be a man of means who could specialise in treating mainly the poorest patients, often for little or no pay. Rumour had it that during his brilliant student days he had attended a rich client in England whom he had saved quite spectacularly from death, and who had rewarded him doubly.

First, he was given an endowment that allowed him to live entirely on the proceeds of the invested money; and secondly he was allowed to marry the client's daughter. She was a charming woman, rumour said, but no beauty; and had eventually sought an amicable divorce when she concluded that Harold Rhone's philandering was more than she wished to put up with. Harold (most acquaintances called him Harry) had been very kind to her, had always been discreet never causing her any embarrassment, and was the perfect lover.

But a woman knows when a man's heart is not entirely hers, and she decided to allow Harry's free spirit its freedom. She loved him too much to imprison him. They had one child, a beautiful girl whom she allowed to stay with Harold Rhone, even when he, after the divorce, decided to return to settle and practise in Guyana.

Few people knew the details of Dr Rhone's life prior to his return to Guyana with his daughter. He never spoke of his relatives, they never visited him, and initially he led the life of a gay bachelor. He was a handsome man, not startlingly good looking, but striking enough to be noticed by women. After a few years of this gay life, however, he got married again, this time to a beautiful woman who seemed to understand him. They had only one child, a son.

Dr Rhone seemed to have a number of widely varied interests on all of which he was well read and current; but there were two which appeared to consume him. One was unceasing work with the poor, including research into the maladies that most frequently afflicted them. On this he wrote learned papers based on his clinical practice, and sent them abroad. Ever so often he would be invited to seminars outside Guyana to discuss those papers, so he became widely travelled. He was a fixture on various Boards of the medical fraternity in Guyana, and rumour had it that he was a high-ranking member of a very powerful lodge.

The other passion was women—not the poor to whom he administered, but the high society females whose boredom he relieved both in and out of their beds, although he never accepted any as his patient. He was invited to all the best parties, was the life of those he chose to attend, and was a good friend and confidante of all the men related to the women with whom he consorted. The men he would treat medically for free, but the women he would simply refer to his medical colleagues in accord with their alleged area of competence. Among his greatest assets was his ability and predisposition to never discuss the women he knew. They could trust him completely to keep their secrets, and therefore told him all, including their cherished fantasies, and gave him unfettered access to themselves. He often satisfied those fantasies.

In relation to men he behaved with equal confidentiality. And that is why Ng Qui Fook told him about Boom Boom, dwelling less on her teeth, and mostly on the other parts of her which he had been privileged to see. His recollections had clearly been enhanced by the repetitiveness with which he had revisited those recollections over the past eighteen months.

Ng Qui Fook's accounts of Boom Boom excited Harry Rhone. He had never seen the young lady, and had not even heard of her before Ng Qui Fook's unburdening of his conscience. Ng Qui Fook simply wanted her as a bed partner; although as time passed he gave up hope. Harry wanted to possess her if she was all Ng Qui Fook said she was. He had recently, in an increasingly compelling fashion, been feeling the need for female companionship with which he could share his work interests. He needed, he felt, a sexually engrossing woman to whose mind he could also relate. He wanted a soul mate, and thought that with the right material he could create one. It had been easy to have that kind of relationship in England, but not in New Amsterdam. He longed for it.

This Boom Boom, about whom Ng Qui Fook had spoken in such great detail, struck him as a kind of female tabula rasa onto which he could write the right information that would make her the soul mate he sought. With a combination of the head on his shoulders and the head on his genitals, he would create his soul mate, catching her before her obviously fertile mind was closed by the influences of New Amsterdam's suffocating parochialism. This rough diamond he would polish into a multi-faceted jewel that would be his!

It was for the purpose of reconnoitring that Dr Harry Rhone proceeded to the drugstore during the middle of that afternoon. In the middle of most afternoons business tended to be slow, especially so on Wednesdays. All the senior staff in the drugstore knew of Dr Rhone, even though few had met him; but Boom Boom was new to the senior staff ranks and had never had cause to be in any discussion about him. When therefore Dr Rhone asked for her, and was shown into her office, she wondered what assistance she might give to this neatly dressed good looking, unassuming man.

He spoke very respectfully but with an easy familiarity to her, and pretty soon persuaded her to call him Harry. He in turn refused to call her Boom Boom, and elicited out of her the name Vlida, which he insisted on using. He had simply said that Vlida was a much more appropriate name for someone in a job as important as hers; and somehow this had pleased Boom Boom.

Almost abruptly he had swung the conversation away from them and had launched into his interests in some new drugs that he had been using to treat hypertension—one of the most prevalent conditions among his patients. Boom Boom had been reading up the promotional literature on some of these new drugs, and had proudly displayed her knowledge. Harry seemed pleased and a little surprised. He ordered some quantities of the new drugs that they had discussed, and then, almost as an afterthought, asked her if it would be alright for him to ask the owner of the drugstore for permission to invite her to a seminar that Harry was holding the next evening at his home for doctors in New Amsterdam and some outlying areas. Boom Boom was so taken off guard that she simply muttered that she supposed it would be alright. Harry immediately left for the owner's office.

Boom Boom sat for a few minutes, pondering what this all meant, and trying to assess what she felt about Dr Rhone. Before she could come to any even tentative conclusions, Dr Rhone and the owner of the drugstore appeared at her office door and the owner was saying that he thought it would be a wonderful opportunity for her to meet some of their more important clients. It's agreed then, Harry said, and turned to leave with the simple throw away remark that the seminar would be at eight in the evening and that it was a totally informal affair so she did not need to dress any more formally than she was dressed for work.

When she got home from work that evening, Boom Boom told her mother about the invitation, and her mother agreed it was a good opportunity for her career. The next day she ascertained that Dr Rhone's house was indeed the large one in the block west of her house, and therefore within easy walking distance.

That evening she bathed early, spent a little more time fixing her face, and put on the simple white dress that her mother had made for her last Christmas. She wore the plain white high heeled shoes she kept for church, and instead of a purse took with her a new leather covered embossed notebook with the pencil in the back that the owner of the drugstore had given her on her promotion. She had never used it because it had seemed too pretty.

At five minutes to eight she knocked on the front of Dr Rhone's house and was met by an elegant lady who introduced herself as Mrs Rhone, and piloted her into the large drawing room in which the seminar was to take place.

Everyone was milling around in a babble of conversations, sipping some drink, when Harry spotted her and Mrs Rhone. He immediately detached himself from the group in which he was and came directly over to her with a loud greeting of *"Ah, here's Vlida, this evening's pharmacist"*. The good-natured, familiar way in which all this was done immediately put her at ease, and pretty soon she was talking with the members of a group to which Harry had introduced her. It was inconsequential small talk which she could follow but to which she did not need to contribute; and it soon ceased as Mrs Rhone brought her something cold and soft to drink, just about the same time that Harry asked all present to be seated as they pleased.

Despite that invitation Harry escorted her to a comfortable chair two seats away from his, next to the only female doctor in attendance. Harry promptly called the meeting to order, and dispensing with all boring introductory formalities, launched into the topic for the evening—the causes, incidence, control, and treatment of hypertension.

This was going to be familiar ground since she had read up all the literature the drug store had on it over the previous day and evening, and had even had a technical discussion with the owner of the drugstore. But she was in for a shock. In ten minutes Harry had covered all the things she knew, and had launched into deeper medical waters, dealing with the peculiarities of Guyanese rural diets and physical life styles and identifying areas of research and consultation that were needed in the field. As he spoke he glanced occasionally at her, smiled a little, and proceeded as if he hadn't done so. After another fifteen minutes, Harry concluded his presentation which he had done without notes, and invited comments and queries from the participants to get a discussion going.

Various doctors made interventions, but even to Boom Boom they appeared trite, repetitive, and not adding any new insights. Suddenly Harry called her name and suggested that she fill the group in on the discussions they had engaged in yesterday about some new drugs coming unto the market in Guyana. Boom Boom nearly fainted, but something about Harry's encouraging smile gave her the courage and confidence she naturally lacked, and before she knew it she was recounting in a clear voice the briefing she had given him in her office. As a matter of fact she improved upon it with some of the information she had read up on afterwards. At the end of her five minute intervention there was clear applause. A series of questions emanated from it and she became the centre of conversation for quite a while. Meanwhile, Harry had moved to the periphery of the group discussing with her and stood there quietly observing the proceedings.

Suddenly, Harry excused himself from the gathering and returned with his wife who promptly served some very fancy looking and good tasting titbits. Another round of drinks and the meeting was at an end. People were beginning to say their goodbyes to the hosts, and Boom Boom took the cue to say hers too. However, when she got to Harry and his wife, Harry simply asked how she was getting home and without waiting for her answer said he would give her a lift home at the same time that he was taking Dr Henderson home. Boom Boom simply stayed silent and waited.

Harry piloted her and Dr Henderson to his car, opened the door for her to get into the back seat, and accompanied by Dr Henderson in front they set off, waved to by Mrs Rhone from the door. Harry had not asked where she lived. He simply drove there. As she opened the door to get out, and murmured her thanks for an enjoyable evening, Harry said he would see her the next day in her office. And then he and Dr Henderson drove off.

She'd got back home around midnight, but couldn't sleep. There was a delayed excitement welling up in her. She had been to her first "High Society" do, had enjoyed it, and had even had a chance to show that she was not simply a pretty, empty-headed, young woman. The doctors there had talked with her like an equal. It was a good feeling to be somebody, if only for a little while. Before she fell asleep, she suddenly remembered John and wondered what he was doing.

Dr Rhone turned up in her office in the middle of the next afternoon. He had two recently published books with him that he placed on her desk with the suggestion that she read them. Then he asked her whether it would be alright to ask the owner for permission to have her work part time with him as his assistant on some research he was doing on the hypertension matter.

He would ensure that she lost no pay, and indeed would pay her separately for the research assistance. Once more she was so taken by surprise that she could only mutter agreement; and he promptly left the office. Later that afternoon, the owner called her to his office to tell her three things. First, that he had heard from several sources about her contributions at the meeting last night and was pleased at how she had performed on behalf of the drugstore; second, that he had agreed to Dr Rhone's proposal that she should for the next six months work in the afternoons with Dr Rhone on his research; and third, that he considered her ready for a pay increase which would commence from the beginning of this current month. More stunning, as he spoke he referred to her not as Boom Boom but as Vlida.

Boom Boom left the owner's office in a daze. She was definitely pleased but apprehensive. She really didn't understand clearly what she was getting into. Nevertheless, she shared the good news with her mother who was equally pleased.

That night, she began studying the books Harry had left with her; and almost fainted with horror. A lot of what she had learnt from the advertising literature on the new drugs was in dispute, and some of the claims had even been refuted. Harry must have known that all along while she paraded her "knowledge". Oh what a fool she had made of herself and how Harry must be laughing at her. She couldn't possibly accept the proposal to work with him!

The next morning she called Harry on the telephone. Before she could say anything about the job, he asked whether she had read any of the books. Her affirmative reply led him to say: *"OK, then you understand why I want you to work for a while with me. I'm writing a book on the need for greater care in the marketing literature about those drugs in small underdeveloped countries like Guyana; and I need you to read and tell me what that marketing literature says."*

She turned up to work at Dr Rhone's surgery just after midday, and found that he had prepared an office for her adjoining his in the surgery. The desk was clear, except for a large paper pad and a stock of pencils; but the bookshelves above the desk had a set of books which he said she had to read to understand what he was working on. Every other day she would spend the afternoon discussing with him one of the books, so she had to read quickly. He had a deadline for preparing the paper on marketing literature. With that he closed the door and left her alone.

For the next six months Boom Boom became completely absorbed in the literature. She could understand it because of her exposure at the drugstore, and in the mornings in between dealing with customers, she read the marketing literature with a keener, more critical eye than before. Life took on a new meaning, even though it meant less sleep, and more study, almost as if she'd gone back to school. There was no heady self-stimulation based on the thrill of scholarship; but Harry encouraged her and she stuck to her task.

Once, she had her period and had failed to complete an assignment. Harry had berated her so badly that she felt terrible and resolved never to let it happen again. He was the hardest taskmaster she ever had, but she liked him and he fascinated her even though she didn't quite share his passion for research. Whenever he travelled, he'd bring her little expensive presents like perfume—not like the cheap ones they sold in the drugstore, but fragrance like those advertised in the chic magazines. Her mother teased her that Dr Rhone was making a pass at her, but she sternly denied it, and she believed her denial.

They worked even on holidays, all day, and she didn't mind not living like "ordinary" young people who were partying and going out all over the place. One holiday Harry took her to an informal official function related to their work, but they left early and at his suggestion went straight to their offices in the surgery.

She'd become familiar enough with him to sit perched on the little bed he used for examining patients, and he had teased her about whether she wanted an examination. In that teasing mood he had walked across to her and kissed her, first quietly, and then more passionately, on her lips. She was taken a little by surprise but responded to his ardour. Soon, he was nuzzling her breasts, and deftly freed them from their bra. The nipples were tantalisingly erect and he teased them with his tongue in the most delightful manner. She felt good, and nestled in his arms as she listened to his soft almost hypnotic voice telling her in a caressing stream of words how much he liked her as a person, and how much he wanted her as a woman.

Imperceptibly, but with great purpose he undid the top buttons of her jeans and pulled them off, leaving her in her soft black lace panties. He clearly liked what he saw and she liked that he liked it. As he stooped to remove her jeans from around her ankles, his lips brushed ever so gently against her upper thighs, and in coming back up he stopped just below her navel and kissed her tummy. She could feel shivers of sensual delight, and closed her eyes with the sensation.

He gently pushed her shoulders down onto the bed and while still fondling her left breast with his left hand, he pulled her panties aside with his right and she suddenly felt the hot warmth of his tongue on her clitoris. She inhaled in a rush of breath and moaned "What are you doing?" But it was a silly question, not really needing any answer other than the increased activity of his darting tongue and warm sucking lips.

She lost all control and simply gave herself up to his ministrations, raising her buttocks to let him take her panties off, and luxuriating in the sensations he was providing. Gently he stopped, just when she thought she would faint with delight, and he kissed her nipples on the way to kissing her tenderly with a long kiss on her lips, teasing her tongue as he did so. Her hands had long gone around his neck, and she could sense him removing his trousers. "Don't you think I'm too hairy?" she asked, in an almost irrelevant way. His answer was a finger assisted hair clearing away insertion of the head of his penis between the lips of her vagina. She tensed up, and squeezed the head with the muscles there at the entrance. His penis quivered, but it stayed erect, waiting for an invitation to proceed, and when he kissed her again and simultaneously gently raised her thighs drawing her towards him, she relaxed and took all of him in a slow long tight entry.

For about half a minute, he simply held that position allowing her to get accustomed to the slight discomfort of his being in there. And then, while still kissing her and nuzzling her ear lobes, he ever so gently began moving his penis backwards and forwards, initially in small almost imperceptible increments.

The sensations were delightful, and sensing that he was looking at her, she opened her eyes. He gazed deeply into them, as he increased the tempo of his movement, slowing at the least sign of pain or discomfort, but persistently, insistently upping the pace. Soon she was reciprocating with her own movements; almost involuntarily following the conductor of the orchestra. She squeezed harder around his neck, buried her lips into his neck under his chin, freed him of the need to support her thighs by clamping them firmly around his waist, and groaned gently as she matched his every thrust. She could feel his balls bouncing against her buttocks with every full thrust, a delight she anticipated each time he partially withdrew, but he was teasing her and sometimes would go only halfway in. Christ, didn't he know that she wanted it all in each time? But he persisted in his teasing half strokes, driving her crazy with anticipated but half fulfilled delight.

Finally she rebelled, grabbed him around the buttocks and drew him fully in, refusing to let him go, but gyrating from side to side as she felt his balls just above her anus, and the pressure of his weight grinding into her clitoris. In a sudden paroxysm of twanging nerves, she let out a loud and prolonged *"Ah-ha-ha-ha-ha-hahhh"*, and clung to him shaking like a leaf in a storm.

When her violent trembling ceased, he gently lowered her thighs, and manoeuvred himself on top of her lengthwise on the small bed, expertly not having his still erect penis slip out. She lay relaxed in this position as he began moving again, this time with urgency, purpose and little gentleness. She felt every thrust as if it was going past her navel, and it excited her all over again. She tried to raise her thighs; but he would only allow her to raise her left thigh, pinning the right to the bed and forcing her to turn on her right side, with her left thigh on his left shoulder.

In that position, with him positioned behind her left buttock but over her right thigh, he reached over and sucked hard on her left breast. At the same time his thrusts became rapid and full, balls swinging on the inside of her right thigh. She couldn't move, but her back arched with each long thrust, and she felt completely invaded.

He seemed intent on plumbing the depths of her and she groaned with gratitude and delight when a long deep thrust paused in the depths and was followed by a quivering ejaculation of warm semen, his penis spasmodically fulfilling its purpose in empathy with her own throbbing vagina.

Slowly he let her thigh down, and then equally slowly allowed himself to settle on top of her side-reclining form. He was heavier than she expected, but she didn't want to move. Most of all, she didn't want him to remove his penis which twitched every now and again, letting go another drop or so. Suddenly, with no conscious control on her part, her own muscles contracted in response to an involuntary cough. Harry's now flaccid penis was expelled, and he muttered in feigned anger "ungrateful wretch" as he laughed and patted her bottom.

They cuddled for a while saying all sorts of silly nothings to each other; but Boom Boom without warning got serious and asked whether Harry did this with all his girlfriends. He replied without hesitation: "Of course not". She looked at him, smiled and said: "Please take me home".

He drove her home, deposited her at the gate, and he watched her go into the house then drove off. In her bedroom a third pair of panties, black lace ones, got added to the bottom drawer of her chest of drawers.

Two weeks later, when they had a chance to be alone in the office, she confided that she thought she was pregnant, and suggested that in all the circumstances she needed to get an abortion. Harry remained quiet for a while, and then agreed. He said he would send her to a reliable doctor for a pregnancy test, and if she was then he would give her the money for the abortion. He himself wished to behave as a layman in this matter.

She was pregnant and did have the abortion. He paid the bill but said he didn't want to know any more details about it. That hurt Boom Boom's feelings, and many years later she would throw it back in his face as evidence of his general uncaring attitude to her.

At the time she was twenty-four, and he was forty-two. The immediate effect of the abortion was to draw them closer together emotionally. He even agreed with her that if she were to get pregnant again, they would not pursue the route of abortion. Their work continued, and eventually she left the drugstore entirely to work with Harry full time as his research assistant. This meant that they spent more and more time together, made love frequently, and were thoroughly happy with each other. She still felt no special excitement about the work itself, but she liked to please Harry. She still had no hobbies and only one long term goal—being accepted into the right stratum of society.

Harry became a regular visitor to Boom Boom's home, and got to know her mother quite well. Her grandmother died not too long after she had become Harry's lover; and her mother, deeming Boom Boom to be quite capable of taking care of herself now, decided to accept her sister's invitation to migrate to the USA to help look after her nieces and nephews.

Boom Boom was left on her own in Guyana. She had no relatives in Guyana with whom she wished to associate closely and regularly; but loneliness was no real problem. Initially it didn't matter. She could now have Harry stay with her at her house without embarrassment, and he did so more and more frequently. Gradually though it became clear that Boom Boom considered the house below her status, and the matter of her moving was settled when the town council deemed the whole tenement yard to be a public health hazard.

Harry helped her find a house. It was less than perfect because it was in a yard with another house in front of it, and even though he arranged for major repairs and furnishings to be done to it, its general and geographical deficiencies were a constant source of carping comment by Boom Boom. It reminded her too much of the tenement yard. But it served as a love nest, and Harry spent many nights there with her, nights always spiced by the most exquisite love making in all parts of the house. She'd cook for him and they would eat and then make passionate love for the rest of the time, even when she had her period.

But problems were looming on the horizon. Harry was always discreet as far as his family was concerned, so he never took Boom Boom to any official functions where the invitations had said "Mr and Mrs". This irked Boom Boom, but she said she understood. The affair continued and got closer. Then Christmas came and Harry found he could not divide himself adequately between his family and Boom Boom. Boom Boom suffered the loneliness of Christmas day in silence, and Harry could find no way to make up for that. The same thing held for Old Year's night.

Harry began to feel miserable because he wanted to be with Boom Boom at those times. He wanted to go to various public places with her. He wanted to take her routinely with him on trips abroad. He had done so once and it had been extremely enjoyable. But he was not yet prepared to take these great steps towards the certain destruction of his marriage. He had a special bond with his wife; and all the other liaisons he had never threatened that bond. They were liaisons with older women, or married women, none of whom really wanted to marry him, possess him completely, or bear children for him. That would have posed as much trouble them as for him, and neither party wished to court that kind of trouble.

But Boom Boom was different. She did want children. She did want Harry to herself, a final public confirmation of her and her mother's dreams about social status. The status of preferred mistress could never be satisfactory. It was the emotional equivalent of the second house in the tenement yard.

Boom Boom, or Vlida as everyone now called her, was Harry's known mistress. Many men envied Harry since she was a fine looking, intelligent woman. But she appeared to be dedicated to Harry. Soon she got a better paying job. She had applied for it with Harry's encouragement. He, knowing how important it was to her to feel that she had achieved things on her own, never mentioned the part he had played in her getting the job. In any event, she merited it in her own right.

Similarly, when an overseas training opportunity arose, he ensured that her being chosen for it could never be traced to his intervention. A year later, when she returned, she appeared still very much in love with Harry, and they even settled back into their lovemaking ways with even more zest. But Vlida's frustration and discontent were increasing with every increase in satisfaction she achieved. She was a victim of the principle that dissatisfaction is satisfaction's child.

With her extra training, job promotion came and she became financially independent enough to move to a house in its own yard. Harry had noted with a resigned shrug that the room dubbed the study remained, as in all her previous homes, simply a storeroom for books, papers, and extra shoes and clothes which she collected in profusion. She barely read parts of books he bought as presents for her. Still, she had no hobbies, no non-self-centred interests, and her interest in non-material things never flowered. She shrieked shrewishly at the maid, and paid no attention to Harry's comments about being a snob.

But for Vlida all material things were working out fine. She got a car, three television sets (one each for the bedroom, the sitting room, and the kitchen), and several other trappings of prosperity and social status. She made frequent business trips abroad. She was a fine looking, well-dressed woman, even better looking than the ones her mother used to sew for. But the one thing she keenly felt she did not have was her own personal man, available to her all the time on all holidays, including particularly Christmas.

By the eleventh year of their affair, when the digits of their ages were once again the same but reversed, Vlida told Harry she no longer loved him. The magic, she said, had disappeared. She was tired of the rut in which she was. He just could not, or was not prepared to, give her the one set of things she wanted most—her own man, children with that man, and a family life that would establish her as a pillar of society.

She was tired of lonely Christmases. She was tired of early morning departures from her bed. She loved children and wanted her own. She wanted, she said, to have some of the good things in life, to travel with her man, to appear in public freely with her man. She had achieved much, but these Harry could not provide. Age wise, time was running out on her. The bond with Harry had to be broken.

Harry was broken. He had not felt so alone, abandoned, and rejected since both of his parents had died in an accident when he was nine years old. He discovered the truth of

Ovid's statement that *"nothing is stronger than habit"*, and Vlida had become his habit. It was the first time that he had understood the true feeling of addiction. He was addicted to Vlida, and she was not to him. Stronger forces prevailed over her feelings.

He could not handle the addiction by simply going into the arms of any of the many other women to whose beds he still had access. A few whom he knew really well in his high-society set teased him about his pining for Vlida. They told him that any woman for whom a man had done as much as they thought he'd done for Vlida, who then behaved the way she did, wasn't worth it. Certainly, they had no respect for her. But Harry just would not entertain discussion on the matter. The bolder ones teasingly offered to fuck some life and sense back into him; and he knew they could. But he also knew that his real loss was that of a would-be creator whose act of creation had gone awry, and mere fucking could not compensate.

His attempts to fill the Boom Boom bill by progressively spending more time sleeping out at her had been like water off a duck's back as far as Boom Boom was concerned—he still went back to his wife. Harry's marriage disintegrated. He lost his exhilaration for living. He moped, brooded, and felt betrayed. And maybe he was; but he recalled one of the moral Maxims of his favourite philosopher from his university days—Francois, Duc de La Rochefoucauld: *"A man who is ungrateful is sometimes less to blame for it than his benefactor".*

Postscript

The last time the high society world of New Amsterdam paid any attention to the Boom Boom and Harry affair, they heard that Boom Boom was having great fun on the international circuit. She hadn't yet fulfilled all her aspirations but she appeared well on the way there. Whether she would be happy when she did, no one could guess; but who cared? Harry did. He would always love the Vlida he first knew. He would always care about what became of the new Vlida. She was the best lover he'd ever had in three decades. He would always poignantly remember the firm voluptuous body that had learnt so well how to please a man sexually, and to derive pleasure from him. But he had played God, had tried to fashion a human being after his own image and likeness, and broken too many of God's and his own rules.

For Harry, he was made of stern enough stuff to remember a passage from Ernest Hemingway's: A Farewell to Arms. That passage said ***"The world breaks everyone and afterward many are strong at the broken places"***. His marriage survived, sort of, and so did his interests in life and in women; but he doesn't play God anymore. He even sometimes hopes that a miracle would occur and Vlida would come back to him. John is an architect.

HARRY'S PLAGIARISED ODE TO VLIDA

Nobody knows you,
You don't know yourself,
And I, who am half in love with you,
What am I in love with?
My own imaginings?

D.H.Lawrence-The Evening Land

THE CONQUERING OF IMO

In 1670, the year during which Charles II was King, the English Parliament passed an Act. The substantive part of its text was as follows:

> **"[Be it resolved]** *that all women, of whatever age, rank, profession, or degree; whether virgin or widows; that shall after the passing of this Act, impose upon and betray into matrimony any of His Majesty's male subjects, by scents, paints, cosmetics, washes, artificial teeth, false hair, Spanish wool, iron stays, hoops, high-heeled shoes, or bolstered hips, shall incur the penalty of the laws in force against witchcraft, sorcery, and such like misdemeanours, and that the marriage, upon conviction, shall stand null and void."*

Imo had never read that Act, and she knew nothing about it; but she lived her life as though she had, and as if it were applicable here in Guyana.

Imo was one hundred and eighty pounds of not unattractive, five foot, seven inch, wide mouthed, open teethed, rotund tight-backsided, dark velvet-skinned, natural woman. She was physically fit, sturdy, compact, and certainly not in need of foundation undergarments, as her flat tummy testified. And her teeth were in perfect condition. She was a respected senior nurse at the Best hospital, had just celebrated her fortieth birthday, and had with great concern just discovered her first grey pubic hair.

The morning when she had made the discovery, she had got out a hand mirror, and had sat quietly for about fifteen minutes examining that part of her to check whether there were any companions of that hopefully solitary harbinger of old age. She could not help focusing on the wider picture; and in her mind there occurred the same thoughts that had motivated Shakespeare's Parolles (in the comedy All's Well that Ends Well) to say: *"Your old virginity is like one of our French withered pears; it looks ill, it eats drily".*

At forty, Imo was truly a virgin in the purest sense. No man had ever managed to even caress her there. She was aware of the truth of Aldous Huxley's pronouncement that *"People will insist . . . on treating mons*

Veneris as though it were Mount Everest"; and had ensured that no would-be conquerors prevailed. She resolved that the time had come to change all that. She was going to get married! A suitable conqueror had to be found.

The trouble with ageing is that as one gets older, unless one loses one's curiosity and ability to acquire knowledge and assess it, one becomes cynical. And cynicism destroys the state of mind required for "falling in love". She wanted a good man whom she could basically control, and who would stay with her because she treated him well. She knew just such a man.

Rupert Oglive lay in bed in Best, in the final stages of recuperation from tuberculosis. When he had first been admitted, he was a rake of a man whom few gave much chance of recovery. About the only un-emaciated thing about him at that time was his thick, seven-inch, flaccid penis which even in its repose exuded a certain pride of being alive. The junior nurses had joked about it, and Imo, at that time to protect poor Rupert from unhelpful embarrassment, took over the duties of looking after Rupert.

He had been a co-operative patient, never making any overbearing demands, even when his illness seemed to be getting the upper hand, or when everyone knew that the food served had been unpalatable. He was a model patient, and appreciated the special attention Imo gave him. He wanted to live.

After a few months of Imo's special care, he took a turn for the better. The doctors were surprised, but all the tests showed him to be well on the way to complete recovery. They all swore that it was Imo's expert, patient, and persistent ministrations that had made the difference and a few told Rupert so confidentially. As he grew stronger, he began to talk to Nurse Imo about himself.

He liked to read spy stories, and she used to bring spy novels from her own collection for him to read. It was through her that he acquired and read all of the Ian Fleming James Bond series. He spoke about his previous work as a cabinet maker, and soon confided that he really had no living close relatives. He had lived on his own, had worked hard at his cabinet making, and clearly had not looked after his health very well. He was a soft spoken man, noticeably imbued with a tenderness and sensitivity not often found in men of his calling.

Recently, there had been one embarrassing incident for him. He had been reading a sexually stimulating part of *"The man with the golden gun"* when Nurse Imo had come to sponge him. He didn't have time to adjust his mind before Imo had removed his pyjama trousers, and he had presented her with his fully erect penis. Flaccid seven had become erect ten and a half. He was forever grateful to Nurse Imo when, with an interesting smile on her face she had simply said: *"I see you're feeling better this morning. Did you sleep well?"* Those quiet matter-of-fact words had been like an instruction to his penis which had promptly subsided into decency. Sponging took place as if the incident had never occurred.

Imo had gone back to her office after attending to him, and had sat quietly remembering his erect penis. She wondered whether Rupert knew how well endowed he was by way of comparison with many other men. He had not been circumcised; but his mother had obviously worked on ensuring that the foreskin could move back freely. In the erect state it did, revealing a smooth, large, spread out King Cobra type head, lighter in hue than the thick shaft which supported it. She knew from practical experience that he was in the top ten percentile.

The only difference the incident seemed to make was that Imo gave instructions that Rupert was now well enough to sponge himself daily; and thenceforth so he did. But Imo still visited him to talk to him and give him his medication. The incident had occurred just before she had discovered the sole grey hair; and she could never be sure that the choice of Rupert as the man she was going to marry wasn't in some measure influenced by it.

The day before he was released from Best, Rupert asked Nurse Imo whether he could visit her after his release. She paused a while before answering, but then said yes and gave him instructions on how to reach her home, and her telephone number. She was off duty on the day he left so he never said a real goodbye.

One week later, her phone rang. It was Rupert. Early the next evening he visited her home for the first time and there began a series of regular visits. Always, he came early in the evening and left after an hour or so. They drank coffee, spoke of all sorts of little personal things, sometimes about novels and films, and about Rupert starting up his cabinet making business again. Eventually he asked how come she had never got married. Imo had simply said that she had not met the right man, and Rupert, with what for him was a rare show of aggression, asked whether she would not consider him the right man. Imo did not reply.

Two weeks later, Rupert reminded her of the question, and this time she answered with her own question. Was Rupert being serious, or just curious? He replied that he was serious, that he wanted to marry her, that he had come to that conclusion even before he had he had left the hospital, and that he hoped she would say yes. Imo looked at him silently for a long time and then said *"Yes. When?"*

The wedding took place in Georgetown three months later; and they went to honeymoon, for one weekend only, in the country at the home of a schooldays friend of Imo. The friend, her husband, and their eight year old son had attended the wedding, and had themselves arranged to stay with friends in Georgetown for the weekend. They had asked their maid, Pearl, to stay at the house during that weekend so that Imo and Rupert would not have to do any cooking or other household chores during their honeymoon.

Around ten that Saturday morning after the Friday afternoon wedding, a policeman turned up at the place in Georgetown where Imo's friend and family were staying. He brought a message from Pearl which simply said that they should come home as soon as possible, since Imo and Rupert were both very ill.

The friends cut short their stay, caught a bus and headed back to home in the country. They got there near midday, and found Imo sleeping while pyjamaed Rupert was sitting listlessly in a rocking chair on the verandah. The husband could not get any sense out of Rupert whose thoughts seemed far away, and the wife did not wish to awaken Imo. So she spoke to Pearl, a young unmarried woman in her mid twenties, who had one child and who could not suppress her laughter as she was asked about what had happened.

With rustic candour, Pearl told the story, introducing and later concluding her account with a phrase that captured what for her was the most significant fact. *"Mrs., he cock big, big, big."*

Pearl said that they had turned off all the main oil lamps and had gone to bed, shortly after Imo and Rupert had arrived. A small lamp had been left burning in the bedroom that Imo and Rupert were to use. About a half hour after Imo and Rupert had retired, Pear, who was lying on the bed in the adjoining bedroom, had heard low voices which had suddenly risen in pitch when Imo started saying quite loudly: *"Wait, Wait, Wait, Oheeeeeee."* That had been followed by a sound of tearing of cloth, and then there was a loud thump like someone falling off the bed. She could then hear Rupert's voice saying *"Oh shit, ah nearly break me hand!"* A brief silence followed, but that was itself soon followed by Imo's irritated and loud admonition couched in ungrammatical English that she never used: *"Rupert, man you gwine sprain me leg. Tek it easy."*

Apparently, Rupert had not obeyed, because Imo had screamed: *"You gwine split me in two!"* There was the sound of a hard cuff, and then the sound of someone falling off the bed again, only harder this time. Rupert's enquiry of: "Woman what wrong with you?" was followed by the sound of a slap, more tearing of clothes, and Imo hollering: *"Jesus Christ, a done for, you gwine shift me womb an' kill me."* Then an honest to goodness fight broke out.

The adjoining wall shook as their two bodies slammed into it. Deep grunts were coming from the room, and suddenly the door of the bedroom burst open as Rupert was flung against it and staggered into the dark sitting room where Pearl was busy trying to light one of the larger kerosene lamps. She had just managed this when she saw Rupert's naked bony frame emerge, and in the flickering light of the just lit lamp she flinched at the size of his erect penis. She could empathise with Imo's protests.

Rupert was obviously embarrassed by Pearl's presence, and although she also recognised that he had a large swelling on his face, probably from a cuff, she dashed into the room to Imo. Imo was sitting on the bed, nightgown torn half off, her large breasts heaving with her sobs, and her hands cradled over her crotch.

Imo cried uncontrollably, and then suddenly lapsed quite. She had fainted, and that is when Pearl got really worried. Pearl got some smelling salts from the medicine cupboard, and when that had revived Imo she set about making some ginger tea. While the tea brewed she fanned Imo with an old newspaper, and generally calmed her down. Pearl ensured that Imo drank the whole cup of tea, and left her only when she appeared to have gone to sleep.

As Pearl went out the door she saw Rupert in a huddle on the floor. He too had fainted. Smelling salts, fanning, and more ginger tea did the trick; and

Pearl noticed that even in his unconscious state his penis hung like a large weapon that did not belong to him. She left him on the floor once she had revived him and given him the ginger tea, and went back to her bed. She could think of nothing else to do.

But three things did occur to her as she mused over the events so far. The first was a medical opinion: *"Rupert mus a de faint cause de blood run outa he head to fill up he cock"*. The second was an organisational conjecture: *"she wish she coulda see how maaga maaga Rupert mus a been like kiskadee pon cow back before he get trow off"*. The third was an emphatic reaction: *"If she was Miss Imo she woulda done get up an haul she arse an gone like fiah movin thru cane piece. Even doh she name woulda gone abroad, talk name doan kill. Nuttin like he coulda ketch she again till fowl get teeth. Man, Rupert mek she own man pass fo grass"*.

Just before foreday morning Pearl came awake to the sounds of more scuffling. This time she could not contain her curiosity, so she stood on a chair peeping over into the bedroom. Apparently Rupert had recovered enough to try to complete the task he had started earlier in the night. Imo was lying quietly but awake on her back, and Rupert, mistaking that for simple acquiescence, hiked her torn nightgown up to her waist. Kneeling between her parted thighs, and erect penis in hand, he prepared to launch another assault. The dim kerosene lamp threw grotesque shadows of the whole scene on the wall and made it look more ludicrous than it was; and Pearl giggled softly with not a little excitement and anticipation of seeing that large penis go in.

But this was no joke, and Imo seemed ready for Rupert. As his penis touched her and Pearl gasped with anticipation at the sight, Imo raised her parted thighs slightly to see if that position would make life less uncomfortable and less painful. It did assist entry, but the sudden exponential increase in pain made Imo reach for Rupert's penis with a view to plucking it out. That penis seemed to have a mind of its own; and as she lost the battle of eviction, her hand slipped to its base and on to Rupert's balls. With groaning rising desperation, rather than malice aforethought, Imo grabbed his balls pulling and squeezing for all she was worth.

Rupert screamed *"Oh Lawd, God"*, fainted once more, and again fell off the bed onto the floor. Imo herself nearly fainted from the sudden relief.

Pearl fell off her chair, not unaware of her own moist crotch, and dashed across to the bedroom.

This time both Pearl and Imo administered to Rupert with the smelling salts and the ginger tea; and that is when Imo agreed for her to send the message with the police. Pearl's preference had been to call the police and get them to lock up Rupert; but Imo had insisted otherwise. Pearl concluded that *"dis married ting was one load o rass if you had fo put up wid all dat"*.

In the cold light of day, the marks on Rupert of the previous evening's mayhem were quite apparent. The swelling of Rupert's face hadn't quite gone down, and his left eye was still almost swollen shut. Imo's friend had persuaded Imo to subject herself to an intimate examination, and, apart from some clear bruising, not much physical damage seemed to have been inflicted by Rupert.

These examinations were followed by a conference between Imo's friend and her husband. They decided on a course of action. The husband would talk to Rupert, and she would talk to Imo. Then they would both talk to the two of them together.

The conference yielded the result that separately and jointly Imo and Rupert said they still loved each other; Rupert understood that he had to be gentler; and Imo understood that she had to be more tolerant of the initial pain and discomfort. About the size of Rupert's penis, about which Imo openly complained both when alone with her friend and when they all met together, it was agreed that nothing could really be done, other than Imo learning to relax a little more.

Her friend's husband had come up with the self-serving idea that maybe he should "prepare" Imo for Rupert, but one look from his wife soon put a stop to his pursuit of that suggestion. Instead, they settled simply for the idea of Rupert and Imo quietly going to sleep for the rest of the day, and them trying the whole exercise that night with the help of the jar of Vaseline that her friend's husband produced. She recommended the Vaseline highly to Imo, saying that it had worked well when she and her husband had tried some sexual variations.

That night, freshly showered, Imo and Rupert approached each other and what they were going to do with great trepidation, but with trust and resolve. Imo, in particular, felt she had to make this thing work. Her pride was involved. In any case how could you control a man whom you couldn't fuck? Rupert's balls still hurt, and Imo still felt sore between her legs. It had smarted when she had gone to urinate. Her friend's husband had made some suggestions privately to Rupert about foreplay and the benefits of saliva delivered with one's tongue to certain parts; and in the new mood of trust and joint endeavour Imo had let Rupert follow the suggestions.

By the time they had got to the Vaseline application stage, Imo was feeling quite relaxed and excited, and they together applied the Vaseline. She, following her friend's advice, put herself in a position where she could control both the pace and the degree of Rupert's penetration; and the sounds which came from their bedroom that night, at least initially, were the right sounds of the successful pursuit of sexual pleasure.

Just listening to them made her friend and her husband get excited, and start their own lovemaking, when suddenly Rupert started hollering— something incomprehensible about Imo squeezing his balls with all her weight, just before he fainted again. More fanning, more smelling salts, and more ginger tea, were administered but this time to Rupert alone.

The next day they had to leave since Imo had to return to work. Imo seemed quite relaxed and happy. Rupert was a little dazed. But they made a pretty picture of a happy newlywed couple as they joined the bus for Georgetown. Pearl had seen them on the roadside that Sunday afternoon waiting for the bus, and marvelled at how they looked *"like Soorah and Doorah"*. She shrugged her shoulders and thought: ***"Every mouldy biscuit gat he own voom voom cheese"***.

POSTSCRIPT

Rupert and Imo lived happily for about two years after which Rupert had a repeat of his tubercular infection. This time, Imo's best efforts did not suffice to stop him passing through death's door. Her friend's husband visited regularly on Saturday afternoons, to cheer her up, and pretty soon Imo was back to her chirpy pre-funeral self. After a while she started to use make-up and to 'press' her hair. She looked different, but she never got married again. Saturdays became her best days.

THE MAKING OF AN ENTREPRENEUR

The room was stuffy, even though they had prohibited smoking. It was almost as stuffy as the lecture which the fellow with two PhDs at the podium was giving. Lonnie "blue" Johnson sat at the back of the room vaguely listening to what was being said. Ordinarily, he would have got up and left, not caring whether anyone noticed; but this time he stayed. After all, it was his money that had financed the whole seminar, and he'd be damned if he wasn't going to get at least a cup of his own paid for coffee at the break.

Blue, as everyone called him, never failed to marvel at the practice of asking someone who'd never run anything but himself to lecture to people, including businessmen, about how to be an enterprising businessman. What's more, usually the lecturers were not good examples of people who had much money, and in these radical days they always looked scruffy, even if the look was contrived. But he'd had his own reasons for agreeing to sponsor the seminar. They had asked him because he was known to be a successful businessman with wide ranging interests, and was clearly well-off. The expenditure would be a useful tax deduction, and the publicity was good for his business relations, particularly with some foreign investors with whom he was currently negotiating. He could also spot talent among the young people attending by listening carefully to the content and the manner of probing of the questions asked.

As far as Blue was concerned, the prestigious lecturer was talking a lot of sophisticated "bull", the results of recent research which he had managed to persuade some damn fool to publish as a book. It was a little like a man who had never been in a boxing ring holding forth about the principles of boxing to boxers.

Blue himself had learnt what he considered the cardinal principles of business during his youth, and had assiduously practised them in all his activities until they had become second nature to him. This twin doctoral novice was trying to paint some of those principles onto already formed personalities. He would fail because they would remain skin deep, and not become a way of life, a way of looking at the world.

As he thought this he chuckled to himself at some of the memories of his formative years. His reminiscences were interrupted by perfunctory applause marking the end of the lecture and the start of the coffee break. Suddenly he rebelled inwardly. To hell with the coffee and the seminar. He would leave now, and they would all assume he had some urgent business matters to attend to. Blue left with the unceremonious haste and brief goodbyes of a busy important pillar of society. Various officials mentioned to him on his way out how pleased they were that he had taken time off from his busy schedule to listen to the opening keynote lecture. Blue left with a feeling of intense relief.

He undressed a soon as he got home, told the driver to check with his mistress whether she wanted the car for the rest of the day (knowing she would say yes), poured himself a vodka and soda, closed the door to his study, and relaxed completely in short pants in a Berbice chair with his legs spread-eagled on the extended arms. The ringer on the phone was switched off, and he gave himself up to daydreaming about his past.

He remembered how if you played any game with people of equal skill, you'd come out ahead if you had a large enough stake to ride out your losses. He'd learnt this in his marble pitching days. They used to play for buttons, and no matter how good you were you couldn't get into the game if you didn't have the five buttons to put up. Initially, he'd scrape together five buttons and join the game, but he soon learnt that if he wasn't lucky right away he'd have only one game and his buttons would be done. No more play.

Blue had solved that problem by doing two things. First, he spent two weeks of the school holidays practising assiduously in his backyard until he convinced himself that he was the best marbles pitcher in the area. When he relaxed between practise sessions, he single-mindedly collected all the buttons he could find. This included using a razor blade discarded by his father and cutting off all the buttons from laundry left to dry in the neighbours' yards. His own yard he did not touch since there was nothing he feared more than his own mother's wrath, and nothing he respected more than her detective skills.

By the end of two weeks he had collected one hundred buttons. He was ready for the competition. Over the remaining two weeks of the vacation he not only cleaned out the other boys' button resources, but he became a button banker lending his friends buttons to play, and charging interest in buttons on the loans. The interest was higher, the more skilled a player that the borrower was; and no loans were made to players of little skill. They were losers and could lose their own resources, not his. He also never lent to anyone whom he did not think he could beat in a fist fight.

As his button bank grew, he grew more interested in the rate of growth of the bank and less in the sheer joy of winning games of marbles. He still practised, but he restricted his competition to high stakes games which he could set up by teasing other good players by saying he was the best, and working the whole deal up into a kind of neighbourhood championship showdown with much higher stakes than normal day to day games. His skill plus his button resources and his lending practices ensured that his button bank grew enormously.

But he learnt a lesson when once he lost a marbles championship tournament. He only barely lost, but he lost nevertheless, and had to fork out a large number of buttons to the winner. He subsequently won a return match, but the lesson stayed with him. He needed something less risky by which to earn buttons.

The recent visit of a circus put the idea into his head. It was a classic case of recognising opportunity and seizing it. The circus had come and gone but had left a desire among the little children for that kind of excitement. Blue resolved to provide it.

His aunt had a large dog which all the children feared. It was said that the dog was large because it had St Bernard in it. Its deep-throated bark did nothing to reduce the general fear of it. Blue was about the only child who could approach it and play with it. He was often over in his aunt's yard picking some fruit and then selling them to his friends for buttons. Blue knew that the dog, Mus, hated all cats other than his aunt's tabby-cat. He had seen it tear the head off a large tom cat that had dared to get into his aunt's yard, thinking perhaps that it could outrun and out jump Mus. That had been at cat mating season, and the tom cat paid dearly for his prurience.

All these facts came together in Blue's head as a grand plan for a circus. He got some tarpaulin from the scouts and set up a big tent in an open unoccupied plot. They had willingly lent him the tarpaulin since he was himself a cub, and generally they approved of his idea of a local circus. That was his "big top". He then recruited some little boys whose antics would comprise the part of the show as clowns when he got them to put on their own made up costumes. And those boys who could do flips and handstands, and things like that were his acrobats. He taught his little sister to ride the donkey in the adjoining yard standing on its back, and there he had another act. The Old Portuguese man, Mr Joachim, who was always showing little children some magic trick, was persuaded to be the magician for the show.

Blue advertised the show by word of mouth, and got such a good response that he had to schedule the show early enough to have two showings per day. The entrance fee was ten buttons, and each child had to walk with their own seat—a drinks box, a chair, anything to sit on. Many paid in advance to ensure admission, so great was the interest especially since he had spread word that there would be a surprise item.

All the artistes were prepared to perform for free—such was the attraction of stardom.

The day for the show came, and the tent was crowded for the opening show. It all went marvellously well, each act outdoing the previous, and generating round after round of applause. Some difficulties did arise, like when the donkey took fright at the crowd in the tent, brayed loudly, farted, and kicked out with its hind legs, initially refusing to allow Blue's sister to mount it. Blue worked hard to calm both the animal and his sister, and succeeded— and it was all taken as part of the act, worthy of prolonged applause.

Then came the time for the surprise item. Blue had been his own ring master and master of ceremonies. He announced the item, dashed out of the tent, and returned with Mus on a long chain. He tied the chain to the centre pole that supported the tent, and Mus stood there barking and growling at his ferocious best. Then Blue disappeared again. This time he returned with ten little boys, each carrying a closed cardboard box with a long string dangling from each. Blue himself had a big pole which he planted in a pre-prepared hole not far away from the centre pole of the tent. The end of each string was tied to the new pole.

One of Blue's assistants beat a tattoo on a large toy drum, and at that signal the other assistants opened the cardboard boxes and ran away. Out jumped ten stray cats, each doing its level best to get loose, but each effectively restrained by its string. Mus erupted into the wildest roar the audience had ever heard from a dog. Some screamed. All cringed away from the centre of the ring on which in previous acts they had been encroaching. Blue took out a long thin tamarind stick, whooshed it in the air and shouted *"Whaplash"*.

The cats caterwauled. Mus burst into a paroxysm of frothing frenzied barking, and war seemed to have been declared. This was not a scene for the faint hearted, and some little girls started to cry. But Blue as ring master was having his moment of glory near the centre of the ring.

In the exhilaration of the moment, Blue's tamarind whip touched a large tom cat. It spun around and attacked its neighbour which, recoiling from that attack, came close enough to Mus for Mus to snap off his tail. Blood spurted from the severed tail, and this drove Mus really wild. With a surge of strength, Mus pulled down the centre pole and there was a writhing screaming mass of people, cats, and angry dog, all under one tarpaulin on the ground. One little boy got out and left at a dead run hollering and pissing his pants. There were sobs, cries of murder, and implorings to the Holy Trinity of God, Jesus, and the Police.

Really, the donkey was the first to take off. The little boy had been second. And somehow in the melee, the cats had got loose from their strings and they too found their way out in a hurry, led by the one that had lost its tail. Mus emerged, hindered by the heavy centre pole, and had to give up the idea of a cat chase. Blue was the last to emerge, and by time he did, his only companion was Mus. All else, including Mr Joachim, had left as fast as their feet could carry them.

Blue looked around at the wreckage of the tent, and spotted the box in which he had kept the takings of buttons at the entrance. He quietly collected the box, untied Mus from the collapsed centre pole and used a short cut to get Mus back to his aunt's house.

Then he collected the borrowed tarpaulin and went home. There would be no second show. None of those who had prepaid for the second show came to reclaim their buttons; and the whole exercise turned out to be quite profitable button wise. Blue returned the tarpaulin at the earliest opportunity, and refused to answer questions about how the whole thing had gone; but word spread as an intriguingly garnished version of the truth. The word also was that Mr Joachim had to seek medical attention for his heart; and he never spoke to Blue for about a year. There never was another local circus attempt.

The 'financial' success of the circus firmly imprinted on Blue's mind that always there were opportunities to improve one's material situation, if you could only recognise the opportunity and grasp it before it disappeared, or someone else grasped it. He kept looking for such opportunities.

One presented itself when a cousin of his from the Corentyne came to holiday with him. Though he himself had been on the Corentyne, most of his friends had not. Maybe, that is why when his cousin Bruce boasted of how well he could ride donkeys and horses, Blue took it all with a pinch of salt while his friends swallowed the story hook, line, and sinker.

Blue's yard was a rather large one, and several donkeys slept there. All the little boys tended to come from time to time for donkey rides, and his parents did not object. Nobody knew who owned the donkeys, and nobody really cared. What Blue knew was that he could use the circumstance to earn some more buttons. He organised a scheme of donkey races, with the young boys vying for the title of champion donkey rider. Blue never took part in the races, but as organiser he did handle the betting on the races, and soon learnt about betting odds and things like that.

Saturday morning was races morning. The races were laps around the yard. There were sprints (one lap races), middle distance (three lap races), and long distance (six lap) races. Blue himself never bet, but he ran the betting business. He was not putting his resources on any jackass.

However, when Bruce came for holiday, Blue got an idea. He organised the races that Saturday as usual, and during them spread the word about how good a rider Bruce was. Soon everyone was challenging Bruce to race. Blue told Bruce that there was a young jackass that slept under the house; and that it had never been ridden by anyone other than him because it could run so fast that nobody else could catch it. However, he, Blue, knew the jackass and could catch it for Bruce to ride. Bruce agreed that he would race if Blue would give him that fast jackass.

Blue then spread the word as people came to bet that Bruce was going to ride a sprint race on the new fast jackass.

Blue ducked under the house, spoke softly to the young jackass, and cajoled it out into the yard. Then, not letting go of its mane, and patting it and talking to it all the time to keep it calm, he led it to the starting line where Bruce was with the other riders. Blue told Bruce to mount it gently, and Bruce did so while Blue still held it. For that race Blue had someone else handle the betting, and he himself quietly placed a large bet that Bruce would come last. The odds were very long because many had bet that Bruce would win or place in the sprint, what with his Corentyne experience and a fast young jackass.

The race was started on the word "Go" of the traditional "Ready, Steady, Go". In a frenzy of farts and back kicks, the donkeys took off from the far side of the yard. Bruce was already far in front, and the crowd was sure he would win. Unexpectedly, however, as the jackass came towards the house it veered off course and headed straight for the house. At full tilt, never even slowing, it headed for the wall of the house, and just before it hit the wall it slid to its knees and went under to where it was accustomed to sleep. Bruce got scraped off its back because he landed face first into the wall of the house. In fact he was knocked unconscious, and had to be revived by having buckets of cold water thrown on him.

That put an end to the day's racing, and to Bruce's reputation as a master jockey. When all had calmed down, Blue collected his massive winnings. He had learnt and profited from another lesson—the value of information. The whole thing had worked because only he had guessed correctly at the lack of skills of Bruce, and knew the habits of the young jackass.

That matter of the importance of information had swerved him in good stead on several other occasions, like the one when he had bet on hip-shot John to win the Bee-Bop competition. John knew the standard moves, but when he executed them he did so with a novelty and uniqueness born of his deformed hip. The crowd loved it, and all was congratulatory until John insisted that he, not Blue, would go to collect the prize. The crowd nearly lynched John when they realised that all his "shots" were simply emanations of his deformity. But by then Blue had collected his winnings.

As he grew older, Blue realised that these principles could stand him in good stead as he pursued several other objectives. Thus, for instance, he was able to have his first real sexual experience, because he had been able to use information to blackmail the parson's seventeen year old daughter whom he knew very well. The parson lived next door to Blue, who had noticed that his attractive daughter frequently visited the out-house near his fence in the middle of the afternoon, when most adults were away at work, and children could be sure to be at school. He had already left school, having passed his school leaving exams, but he did not yet have a regular job. Sheer fastness made him decide to peep at her one day when he saw her go in there, and he was fascinated to see that her real purpose was masturbation. He confirmed this on the subsequent two days, because she had repeated the exercise.

On the fourth day, he climbed through the fence after she had entered the out-house, and had knocked quietly on the door. Startled, she had murmured "I'll be out just now", and had obviously cut short the exercise to allow whoever wanted to use the place to get in. When she opened the door she saw Blue who smilingly told her what he knew, said he would tell his mother who would tell her mother, unless she went back in and allowed him to have intercourse with her. Neither of them had regretted Blue's blackmail exercise, and the daily mid-afternoon visits continued for quite a while to their mutual satisfaction.

A similar benefit had accrued from information gathering with respect to the Headmaster's wife who was Blue's other next door neighbour. In this case Blue had noted the regularity of the weekday mid-morning visits of a young carpenter to the headmaster's home. By climbing up into the genip tree which overlooked the bedroom Blue had learnt that the carpenter was the wife's lover; and meticulous observation of the kind that any scientist would be proud of taught him sexual techniques he could never have imagined on his own. He promptly put into practice what he learnt in the mornings with the parson's daughter during the mid-afternoon trysts. But his mind also recognised that he had not grasped the totality of opportunities that his new information presented.

He devised a plan. Just before the carpenter was scheduled to arrive, he knocked on the front door of the headmaster's home. The headmaster's wife answered, and Blue said that he had something very important that he wanted to discuss with her. At that point there was a knock on the back door, and they both knew it was the carpenter arriving, although she did not know that Blue knew.

She left to answer the door with Blue saying that he didn't mind waiting. She let in the carpenter, asked him to wait in the kitchen, and returned to Blue to whom she began saying that she would suggest he come back after lunch, since she had a visitor to whom she had to attend right away. Smilingly, Blue suggested that was not a good idea; and before she could protest with the indignation that had already formed in the expression on her face, Blue said some things that made her realise that he was very familiar with the details of her lovemaking with the carpenter. Her mouth fell open with consternation, and she did not hesitate to accept Blue's suggestion that she send the carpenter away.

Blue could see the befuddled carpenter go through the gate (he would have given anything to know what she had told the carpenter); and then he proposed that if she did not want him to arrange for the Headmaster to know what had been going on, she should let him take the carpenter's place this morning. She looked at him quietly for a brief while, and then said "OK". It had occurred to her that with so young and inexperienced a boy, she could quickly satisfy his sexual desires and get rid of him. After all, no youngster like him could deal adequately with an experienced thirty-nine year woman like her; and she would later work out what to do about him.

She led Blue into the bedroom like a lamb to the slaughter; and seductively undressed, stopping at her panties, since she had worn no bra anyway. Blue's heart was beating like a drum, but he kept his cool. Though her body was far more exciting than that of the parson's daughter, he had a plan and would stick to it. He touched her in the places and in the way he knew from his peepings that she preferred to be touched, and she was so pleasantly surprised by his expertise that she entered fully into the spirit of things, secure in the knowledge that her reciprocal ardour would soon be Blue's undoing.

By the time Blue had removed his own clothing not without more than a little help from her, he was ready to put the second part of his plan into action. He executed a sequence of lovemaking that represented her preferred positions and sequence of positions, but with one important difference. He never ejaculated, and thereby presented her with ever increasing stimulation in a way the carpenter had never done. It was like a seamless construct of music with one movement fusing into the next without pause—a medley of ever increasing delight.

Stamina and youth were on Blue's side; but that pair did not explain things completely to her. She decided that she had to wrest control from this young but pleasing upstart, because her husband would soon be coming home for lunch.

Something unusual was called for; and so without hesitation she wriggled his penis out of her and with a swift sure movement took him into her mouth while she simultaneously caressed his scrotum with both hands.

Blue went into spasm and ejaculated, just as she let out a stream of curse words as she pulled the shoelace he had tied around his balls to inhibit orgasm.

Suddenly she stopped being angry and laughed. She had never come across anyone who had done that. Blue himself would never know whether there was good anatomical reason or merely mind over matter that made it appear to work. He simply accepted her advice as an older woman that he should never do that again if he did not want to injure himself permanently. They became good friends, Blue visited from time to time, and the carpenter lost his job.

A knock on the door of the study aroused him from his reverie. It was the maid saying that a young lady was here to see him. He did not recall having arranged any appointment with any young lady for today. Ordinarily, he would have testily told the maid to ask the young lady her name and suggest that she make an appointment through his secretary in the office. But his reminiscences had put him in a good mood, so he issued instructions for the young lady to be shown into his study. Meanwhile he had started thinking of the futility of a lecturer trying to teach in lecture-note form the principles he had imbibed and practised since his youth.

As he rose from the Berbice chair, his heart skipped a beat. There, standing in the doorway of the study, was the parson's daughter. It was unmistakably she, even though some fifteen years had passed since those out-house episodes. He smiled at her, said how pleased he was to see her after all these years, and asked where she had been and what she had been doing.

It turned out that among other things she had gone abroad to university, had been for the past two years working for a large manufacturing firm, and had noticed him when she had attended the seminar that she knew he had sponsored. When they had broken for lunch she had set out to find him and had learnt from his office that he had probably gone to work at home. So here she was.

Blue was familiar with the word and the concept "serendipity". He wondered what to make of this opportunity.

POSTSCRIPT

Blue had never married. He'd always been too busy figuring the angles, grasping the opportunities, and a family would have diverted him from the dollar equivalent of his youth's button collection. The parson's daughter changed all that, especially after his mistress had arrived unexpectedly and had created a vulgar scene about the fact that he had picked up from where he had left off in the out-house fifteen years ago. She thought the parson's daughter was a new woman he had picked up, and reacted inappropriately. She didn't have the right information.

AN INSTITUTIONN OF BYGONE DAYS

Clickiticky—Clack, Clickiticky—Clack, Clickiticky—Clack, Clitick, Clitick, Clitick, Clitick, Clack. This was the syncopated, onomatopoeic, contribution of the East Coast railway train to the delight of the little children who lived close to the railway embankment. Several times per day it provided the calypso type rhythms to which they would dance with varying degrees of vulgarity and nudity as the train passed. This impact crossed ethnic barriers as the tracks moved through one ethnic community into another. No one in 1846 would have thought about this when work had begun on the first railway in South America, from Georgetown to Mahaica.

That railway had become an important social institution. It did not simply carry passengers and goods as had been intended between all the villages from Georgetown to Mahaica. That was its mundane purpose. Its far more sophisticated reality was its impact on social life.

On Easter Monday and on other similar national holidays it featured in out of town picnics, with the most popular carriage being the one in which the dance band was. Churches and other less religious groupings all availed themselves of this facility. It spawned and supported the institution of "fried fish and bread" at Mahaica.

It determined the wake-up hours of hundreds of children who rode the first train to high schools in Georgetown, and of adults who lived in the country and worked in the town. For this captive subset of "first train" determined risers, the train schedule determined a whole range of domestic activities within their households—Fetching water from the afternoon or night before to ensure availability for bathing and cooking the next morning, often before sunrise; For men and boys "pressing" trousers by laying them under the mattress the night before so the seams were sharp the next morning; For girls, plaiting hair and tying it in an old stocking the night before bedtime to facilitate grooming early the next morning.

Even the domestic animals were affected. For many children, feeding the fowls or looking after the pigs were chores that had to be completed before preparing for school and catching the train. Many a rooster had his traditional role stolen from him by this intrusion on the sequence of waking up.

Often, particularly for those living furthest from Georgetown, homework was done on the train, so the carriage became a study. And for those who weren't catching the train, those who were served as human alarm clocks. If they were running to get to the train station it meant that it was late. If they were sauntering it meant it was early. The plaintive remark: *"It early ma, da girl na ah run"* was an acceptable rebuttal of a young child being hurried up about morning chores by an over-anxious mother.

The train fostered the development of a whole range of careers associated with its operation—flag waving, whistle blowing conductors and ticket collectors; station masters; engine drivers; porters; and charwomen, to name a few. It confused young children about careers, forcing teachers in schools to explain that an engineer was not an engine driver. It stimulated poetic endeavour as people yielded to the urge to endow the train engines with a personality, and gave them names like "Sir Donkey" on the basis of their perceptions of the power and speed of the iron monsters.

The last train, the train that left latest from Georgetown (around six in the afternoon) was special. More than any other it provided the opportunity for romantic trysts between individuals who otherwise may never have met, let alone courted each other. It was on the last train that some of the most intriguing incidents occurred.

Take, for instance, the case of Maisie Harewood. Maisie was a schoolteacher in her mid twenties who taught at a primary school in Kitty. She lived, however, with her parents in Beterverwagting—BV as it is known—some eight miles away. Rumour had it that her father was a strict old geezer who wouldn't let any man come too close to her. She must have been relieved to work away from home. Those were the days when no decent girl lived away from home if she was unmarried, unless she was living with relatives, and certainly didn't live on her own.

Maisie travelled to work and back home daily on the train during the week. She was the stereotypical "teacher girl", outwardly very prim and proper, neatly but conservatively dressed, and properly spoken. Physically she wasn't bad looking in an overall sense. One would not have been ashamed to take her out.

In a more detailed sense though, she had some flaws. She was slightly knock-kneed; had a little too much bust (40-D squeezed into a 38-C bra) for her barely five foot three height; had slightly too hairy heavy calves and legs which she did not shave; and was endowed with slightly too ample a flat backside whose rotundity seemed to have been transferred to her tummy. It was as if she had an accident in which she had been hit from behind and the bulge there had been rearranged in front. All this was wrapped in a light brown complexion which in those days was a forgiving feature of the flaws.

Ordinarily, Maisie went home on the four-thirty train from Kitty, what with school ending at three. But she acquired an ardent admirer in the form of a young male teacher at the same school. She took to coming to the Kitty train station as if she were coming for the four-thirty train, but deliberately waited with her young man for the last train. They sat at the far end of the station platform, held hands, and spoke lovingly to each other for the whole two hour wait. When the last train came, they waited until the last precious minute to bid each other goodbye, and for Maisie to board the train.

This routine became well established, and the conductor on the last train understood the whole thing as well as did all the older schoolboys who had stayed back to play games at school or just to lime or wait for their own girlfriends. All the last train loved a lover.

The regular conductor, however, went on leave, and his replacement had not been briefed on the routine. So, when the time came for the train to leave Kitty, the new conductor paid no attention to Maisie and her escort, waved his green flag, blew his whistle and signalled the train into motion. Maisie was taken by surprise, and scrambled to get onto the platform of the last carriage. She had to run, and then try to jump onto the platform.

She had seen boys do this often, but had never tried it herself. In fact she considered the exercise rather dangerous, as indeed it was for the uninitiated. But she had to get on that last train!

One of the bigger schoolboys helped by taking her handbag and briefcase. Another grabbed both her arms. Her boyfriend, running along the platform and accelerating in step with the train, reached under her buttocks and pushed from behind while the schoolboys pulled from in front. Her skirt was riding up showing far more thigh and backside than she would have wished, but modesty had to be ignored. Maisie was suspended between the pulling boy and her pushing boyfriend, and just before she reached the end of the station platform, they succeeded in transferring her onto the train.

By that time the train had built up speed, and Maisie's boyfriend was travelling at the speed of the train, looking like Carl Lewis in full flight. But the end of the platform was there, and he couldn't stop. He was no athlete, but like a long jumper he took three long flailing strides in thin air, and then gravity took over. He landed on the lady selling genips and other fruit just below the train station, and as the train disappeared around a curve of track all the passengers on the left side, including the schoolboys and Maisie, burst out laughing as they saw him being assaulted by the surprised, affronted fruits vendor in whose basket he was sitting. You know, *"teeth doan laugh good ting!"*

It was a good eight feet from the platform to the ground, and he must have been terribly bruised. But such is the stimulus to procreation, fed by the view of rounds thighs and a broad arse, that the next day he was there again with Maisie at the Kitty train station waiting for the last train. This time, they did not wait for the last minute for Maisie to board the last train.

But love and the pursuit of carnal knowledge were not the only reasons for taking the last train. For some, having a last drink at the rum shop near the train station was an equally good reason. The shovel-man Harrichand (Harry for short) fell in this category. That Friday afternoon he had more than his fill of brown rum, and it showed in his gait, and sounded in his speech. The train had started to move off as Harry downed his *"one fo de road";* and shovel and canvas bag in his left hand, he ran for and caught hold of the rail on the platform of one of the carriages with his right. There was only one problem. He had caught hold of the wrong rail. One ought to hold the rail that would cause the momentum of the train to swing you onto the platform. The other handrail would cause you to swing in between two carriages. As those near the train windows looked on they beheld the horror of Harry swinging in between the carriages, and swore that he would fall and be crushed by the wheels of the train.

The conductor was among those who had seen Harry's attempt to jump onto the train. He blew his whistle and waved his red flag for all he was worth, and the engine driver heard and saw and braked the accelerating train. As the train slowed down, Harry swung out, and all the onlookers broke into applause of relief. You see, Harry had never let go of the rail, even though it was the wrong one. Harry might have been drunk, but he wasn't stupid. The slowing of the train allowed him to get onto the platform and he climbed up to the top stair and simply sat there, apparently in a daze. No one could get him to move. He had seen death too close up.

Death was a not unknown, but thankfully not too frequent, event associated with the train. Quite often it involved animals which had strayed onto the tracks and had not got out of the way fast enough. When this was the case with a cow, when the "cow catcher" on the front of the engine served its purpose, the people living near the railroad embankment had free meat. No slaughter house ever could do as efficient a job of cutting up a large cow as those people. What they could not use for themselves they routinely sold in the village. And word always spread fast about the availability of such meat. So much so that when instead of a cow, it was a donkey that got killed by the train, the carcass was treated as though it were a cow. Rumour had it that then you got blue beef when it was cooked.

Sometimes though, death occurred on the train itself. Big, fat, bulbous Miss Harris, the Big Market market vendor from Golden Grove, was going back home from Georgetown on the Saturday afternoon two o'clock train. All regular travellers on the train knew her. They knew that her size required her to take up two seats, under which she would push her empty market basket. Ergonomics was still a nascent science that had not invaded the construction of seats on the train. When the basket was full she would put it in the van at the back of the train, but when it was empty it stayed with her. They also knew that it was better to let Miss Harris have the two seats if that were at all possible, since if she was squeezed into using only the one seat she had paid for, the hapless occupant next to her would be subjected to a near endless stream of silent but potent farts and loud belches that she apparently could not control in that state of compression.

Often, the older children would speculate that all her underwear must have been homemade, since no store stocked the sizes she would need to wear; and the older boys marvelled at her thin husband who had caused her to father some ten children, it was alleged. Everyone called her Miss Harris, in defiance of custom about married women, maybe because they had decided that she was the dominant partner in a common law union. Mr Harris was a small wiry man who always sat opposite her when he travelled with her on the train; but today he was not travelling with her.

All went well with Miss Harris until the train got to Enmore, when a thin dhoti clad East Indian man joined the carriage. The only seat available was next to Miss Harris, and the poor fellow forced his way into the window seat next to her. Half of Miss Harris' left buttock hung over the aisle and she was obviously upset. Nevertheless, she said not a word until, as the train came around a bend, the East Indian man lurched against her.

That was the limit. She unceremoniously shoved him upright, and let go some choice expletives about how he better keep himself straight. The train went around another bend of track, and the man lurched over onto her again. This time she threatened to slap him, and the general commotion was such that the conductor who was in the carriage came across to see what was going on. He asked the East Indian man for his ticket, but got no reply. Miss Harris launched into a tirade about these *"tiefing coolies"* who want to ride free on the train, and only making people uncomfortable.

The conductor ignored Miss Harris and reached across to wake the East Indian man who seemed to be sleeping. As he touched the man, the man slumped forward, and the conductor realised that something was dreadfully wrong. In fact, he was sure the man was dead, and made the mistake of muttering so to himself, loud enough for Miss Harris to hear. The scream Miss Harris let out attracted the attention of the whole carriage. The conductor became really convinced the man was dead since he had not stirred even after that scream.

In a flash Miss Harris was up and running to the door of the carriage, as far away from the seat as she could get, but not so far away that she could not see what was going on. Indeed, the East Indian man **was** dead. They lifted him off at Golden Grove, and the stationmaster called the police. Miss Harris left the train at that station, without her basket which she didn't bother to go back for. Rumour soon had it that it was Miss Harris' farts that had killed the East Indian man, and she never again had any trouble getting two seats to herself.

There is no longer any East Coast train. Many of those who rode it have themselves passed away; but a few remain who have fond and sometimes amusing memories of that institution of bygone days.

POSTSCRIPT

The first journey of the train on the East Coast railway must have been quite an event, viewed from the vantage point of the human and animal populations along the embankment. Quite what the stray dogs, fowl cocks, cows, horses, and donkeys thought would make an interesting story if only it could be ascertained and told. Equally fascinating, but in a different sort of way, would be the facts related to the allegation that the women of Buxton had stopped the train carrying dignitaries many years later.

EULOGY FOR A WHORE

She belonged to an era and a class for which a soubriquet was the rule rather than the exception. The wisdom of parents in naming the accidents they called their children was overruled by the realities of those children's actions. Even the law recognised this phenomenon through its frequent use of "a.k.a". Aliases were better carriers of information than baptismal names, since the former derived from reality while the latter merely represented hope, often forlorn, as in the case of "Saint Names".

Compare, for instance, "Big Tom Puss" and "Lil Tom Puss" with "Peter" and "John", two brothers who specialised in stealing 180-pound bags of rice; or "Crotch Cannibal" with "Matthew" whose specialty doesn't bear mentioning.

"Cocka Wally" and "Guy Monkey" were the proud possessors of large penises; "Chucks" was a dice player; and "King Pope" was a fellow who "poped" so many dances that out of ingrained habit he even poped his own, climbing through a window. "Bus Stop" regularly fell asleep while waiting for the bus, regardless of the time of day or night, and was therefore often late. "Gangasaka's" claim to fame was that he would put a whole fried fish in his mouth and the bones would come out at the sides—his relation with the large house lizard (a gangasaka) was pellucid. Rumour had it that if a Gangasaka held on to you it would not let go until thunder rolled.

Often, tough, the symbolism of a name was obscured by events more famous than those which had given rise to the original name; and direct linkages to physical characteristics mattered less than earned reputations. Thus, while, for instance, "Christmas Bugger" did reflect the owner's preferred Yuletide activity, and "Shorty Moe" was indeed short in stature, Shorty's most famous exploit referred to his fowl stealing activities. He had been challenged while in a fowl coop by a policeman enquiring "Who's there?" and had replied "Us Chickens"—a reply that got him six months in jail.

Similarly, "Bourda Monarch" had as his most famous exploit the circumstance that he was the first man to swear on radio in Guyana. Bourda Monarch had been singing in the talent spotting Radio ZFY song competition, and when they "gonged" him he had spontaneously blurted out: "Oh scunt!" He was banned from ever appearing again. Blood Fish (the barber), Cent Oil, Duck Shit, Rope sole, Joe Young, Wood Head, Cousin Swa (the fisherman), Two cent, and Honours all fell into this category of obscure linkages with their aliases. These linkages were known only to the few.

Not so, however, for "Rat Poison". This popular whore's claim to fame was that a rat had bitten the crotch of her panty and had promptly died. It had been found there early in the morning by a client who had arisen early to leave the room before daylight. The client's comment was the exact replica of Bourda Monarch's when he got the gong; and for three days he found excuses to stay away from his wife while expecting the worst. The worst did not occur; but he spread the word and the soubriquet was established.

Rat Poison was a pretty girl, the kind whom the more naive whoremongers were prone to ask: "What's a nice girl like you doing in this business?" Depending on her assessment of the financial status and gullibility of the questioner, Rat Poison had varying answers. If he appeared financially well heeled, she would break down into tears and sob out a story of being an orphan who is trying to get out and be respectable as soon as she could get enough money to start a little hair-dressing business. For the more romantic sounding types, the story was desertion by an unscrupulous lover who had deserted her after causing her to leave her mother's home. For yet others, she was from a poor family, her father had died, and she was earning money to pay for commercial lessons—shorthand and typing—so that she could get a good job as a secretary. These stories were all part of the service she provided as a sex worker. They weren't lies. They were just part of what the clients wanted to salve their consciences.

Of all the whores, she was the best spoken, correct in her grammar and polished in her intonation when she wanted or needed to be. There was one occasion on which this had got her into trouble. A white foreigner had become so enamoured of her, that he had paid for her outfit and taken her to a high-society function. She was amazed at the number of "respectable" men at that function whom she knew, and knew that she knew better than their wives knew them. The evening was a social disaster since so many of these men were uncomfortable, and avoided her. One particularly impolite bastard had even asked her "what the fuck she was doing here with respectable people".

She had never again gone to one of those functions; but she had got her own back on the impolite fellow the next time he turned up as a client. She had charged him double up front, and had teased him into such a state of prurience that he complied when she insisted he perform cunnilingus on her and then he licked her arse. At that stage she farted in his face and refused to have intercourse with him. She lost a client but regained her pride.

Sunday was her day of rest. On that day she went to church early enough before mass to have her confession heard and get absolution for the past week's sins. She knew her confessor was a poofter; but he had his preferences and she had hers. Often she was intrigued by the detail which he required of her as she confessed; but the detail was required, he had explained, for him to set the penance accurately. The only detail which she refused to give was the names of her clients who preferred anal sex with her; but while withholding the names of what she euphemistically called her "nut-butter clique" she did divulge details of technique and that seemed to suffice. Washed free of sin, and having partaken of the body and blood of Christ, she could launch into the new week rejuvenated.

Rat Poison could empathise with her confessor. Indeed, during her work week she played a not dissimilar role. The economics of her business had gradually led her to restrict her clientele to the upper earning crust of society. She often wondered how all these well-off men had such unimaginative wives. The men confessed their cherished and preferred fantasies to her, sometimes directly in words, and sometimes by indirectly indicating what they wanted; and she almost invariably helped them translate those fantasies into reality. Almost always they indicated that their wives could not, or would not, satisfy those longings. It did occur to her that maybe the men preferred wives like that; but insightful woman that she was, she often thought that if the wives could find the male equivalent of her, they would behave exactly like their husbands.

In fact, she knew of one such case. He was a chauffeur whom she liked and would give a free piece to from time to time, especially since he would run errands for her during his work time. He was providing for his boss' wife the same kind of service she provided for his boss. Rat Poison thought that the wife was getting the better deal, since she was getting it free, and her supplier positively enjoyed delivering the service. In this regard Rat Poison always marvelled at the view which men seemed to have that they were getting something from the woman when they became sexually involved. As far as she was concerned, the chauffeur should have been charging the wife, but typical man, he couldn't see the point. He thought he had a good enough deal with exquisite job satisfaction. Men and women do think differently, she concluded.

As time passed the very likely occurred. Rat Poison picked up an infection from some one of her clients. She had a fair idea who it was, but couldn't be sure. That is why, when she went to the doctor immediately after discovering it, she could not truthfully answer his question about whom she had got it from. Fortunately though, it was one of those irritatingly itchy, runny ones that was classified as a minor STD, and yielded rapidly to the antibiotic injections. Nevertheless, the doctor suggested she abstain for about a month. She did.

Rat Poison seized the opportunity of that month of enforced vacation to visit her mother in the country. The change of scene, she argued, would do her good. In fact, the good it did her was more emotional than physical. For the first time she had a chance to talk to her mother freely on a woman to woman basis. They had never been close, and this was the first time her mother had talked to her about how her father had died. He had been a fisherman, and on that morning he had left after some quarrel with her mother about money. He had, her mother said, not been earning enough and too much of what little he earned was being spent on rum with his fishermen friends. He had left home in a huff, and that was the last she had seen of him. There had been an accident at sea, and his body had never been found.

Though her mother was a young woman, she had never remarried, although she had a series of lovers, some of whom had lived with her for short periods. Rat Poison remembered the succession of 'uncles" she had as a little girl, but only now could really empathise with her mother's position. When things got really financially hard, her mother had sent her to an aunt in Georgetown, who did not treat her well. She had become aware of the potential of the asset between her legs when she had asked a man for money to buy kerosene oil. She had got the money and the kerosene, but had lost her virginity at seventeen against a telephone post in the dark street behind her aunt's house. Thereafter, money was not a problem.

The month in the country with her mother was like going back to a simpler place in time. She could not remember when last she had felt so relaxed. She did many of the things she remembered doing as a little girl, including bathing naked in the rain in the backyard. That proved to be her undoing.

She contracted a terrible cold, left it alone for too long as she and her mother tried home remedies, came down with pneumonia, and died.

Rat Poison had always walked with her savings bank book, which she ensured was updated by the bank each month. Her mother, on looking in it was amazed to see how money her daughter had saved. There was enough to secure her a better than average funeral, and to keep her mother in good condition for the rest of her likely life. She had spoken to her mother about her church going activities and that is what led her mother to visit Rat Poison's confessor. He was sorry to hear of her death and insisted that her funeral service be at his church with him being the officiating priest. All the arrangements were made.

On that Saturday afternoon of the funeral service, most of the women who attended were Rat Poison's fellow sex workers. It wasn't a big funeral. None of her clients attended except one—an old Portuguese man whom she had known for many years, and whom on occasion she had helped out of financial difficulties by lending him money which he always repaid. The chauffeur brought his boss' wife. But all except two of the boys attended. Blood Fish, Cent Oil, Duck Shit, Rope Sole, Big and Lil Tom Puss, Muscle Jaw, Joe Young, Wood Head, Cousin Swa, Bourda Monarch, Two Cent, Cocka Wally, Guy Monkey, Honours, Crotch Cannibal, Chucks, King Pope, Gangasaka, and Christmas Bugger all attended, dressed up in their suits. Bus Stop missed the bus, and Shorty Moe was in jail.

The poofter did the eulogy. Of them all, he was indeed the person who knew Rat Poison best—she had weekly told him all her exploits for the last twelve years. His eulogy was a masterpiece of *double entendre,* as for instance when he referred to Rat Poison by her proper name, which few knew, and described her as *"a woman who had dedicated her life to the happiness of men."* The Portuguese man sang *"Rock of Ages, Cleft for me, Let me hide myself in thee"* with great feeling; and so did all when they rendered *"Amazing Grace"* with the reference to *"saving a wretch like me".*

POSTSCRIPT

Rat Poison died in mid December, and the Christmas feeling was already in the air. Carols were being played on the radio and the countdown of how many shopping days there were to Christmas was a daily feature of the newspapers. After the funeral, Christmas Bugger had sought out the officiating priest to say how much he and his friends had appreciated the priest's gesture of personally handling Rat Poison's funeral service. Before the end of the year they had become good friends and Christmas Bugger became a regular church goer. He even quoted parts of the mass to his friends in Latin.